THE ROYAL HORTICULTURAL SOCIETY
DIARY 2008

Commentary by Brent Elliott

Illustrations from the
Royal Horticultural Society's
Lindley Library

FRANCES LINCOLN LIMITED
PUBLISHERS

Frances Lincoln Limited
4 Torriano Mews
Torriano Avenue
London NW5 2RZ
www.franceslincoln.com

The Royal Horticultural Society Diary 2008
Copyright © Frances Lincoln Limited 2007

Text and illustrations copyright © the Royal Horticultural Society 2007 and printed under licence granted by the Royal Horticultural Society, Registered Charity number 222879. Profits from the sale of this diary are an important contribution to the funds raised by the Royal Horticultural Society. For more information visit our website or call 0845 130 4646

An interest in gardening is all you need to enjoy being a member of the RHS.

Website: www.rhs.org.uk

Astronomical information reproduced, with permission, from data supplied by HM Nautical Almanac Office, copyright © Council for the Central Laboratory of the Research Councils.

All rights reserved. No part of this publication may be reproduced, stored in a retrieval system or transmitted, in any form, or by any means, electronic, mechanical, photocopying, recording or otherwise, without either prior permission in writing from the publishers or a licence permitting restricted copying. In the United Kingdom such licences are issued by the Copyright Licensing Agency, 90 Tottenham Court Road, London W1T 4LP.

British Library cataloguing-in-publication data
A catalogue record for this book is available from the British Library

ISBN 10: 0-7112-2731-4
ISBN 13: 978-0-7112-2731-6

Printed in China
First Frances Lincoln edition 2007

RHS FLOWER SHOWS 2008

All shows feature a wide range of floral exhibits staged by the nursery trade, with associated competitions reflecting seasonal changes and horticultural sundries. With the exception of the shows held at Cardiff, Malvern, Chelsea, Hampton Court, Tatton Park and Wisley, all RHS Flower Shows will be held in one or both of the Society's Horticultural Halls in Greycoat Street and Vincent Square, Westminster, London SW1.

The dates given are correct at the time of going to press, but before travelling to a show, we strongly advise you to check with the Compass section of the RHS journal *The Garden*, or telephone the 24-hour Flower Show Information Line (020 7649 1885) for the latest details.

FRONT COVER *Paeonia villarsii* [identification uncertain]. Hand-coloured engraving after C. Delorme from Alexis Jordan & Jules Fourreau, *Icones ad floram Europae* (1866–1903).

BACK COVER *Campanumoea lanceolata* [now *Codonopsis lanceolata*]. Unsigned hand-coloured engraving from Philipp Franz von Siebold & J. G. Zuccarini, *Flora Japonica* (1835–41).

TITLE PAGE *Campanumoea lanceolata* [now *Codonopsis lanceolata*]. Unsigned hand-coloured engraving from Philipp Franz von Siebold & J. G. Zuccarini, *Flora Japonica* (1835–41).

OVERLEAF, LEFT *Tulipa planifolia* [now *Tulipa gesneriana*]. Hand-coloured engraving after A. Mignol from Alexis Jordan & Jules Fourreau, *Icones ad floram Europae* (1866–1903).

JANUARY

M	T	W	T	F	S	S
	1	2	3	4	5	6
7	8	9	10	11	12	13
14	15	16	17	18	19	20
21	22	23	24	25	26	27
28	29	30	31			

FEBRUARY

M	T	W	T	F	S	S
				1	2	3
4	5	6	7	8	9	10
11	12	13	14	15	16	17
18	19	20	21	22	23	24
25	26	27	28	29		

MARCH

M	T	W	T	F	S	S
					1	2
3	4	5	6	7	8	9
10	11	12	13	14	15	16
17	18	19	20	21	22	23
24	25	26	27	28	29	30
31						

APRIL

M	T	W	T	F	S	S
	1	2	3	4	5	6
7	8	9	10	11	12	13
14	15	16	17	18	19	20
21	22	23	24	25	26	27
28	29	30				

MAY

M	T	W	T	F	S	S
			1	2	3	4
5	6	7	8	9	10	11
12	13	14	15	16	17	18
19	20	21	22	23	24	25
26	27	28	29	30	31	

JUNE

M	T	W	T	F	S	S
						1
2	3	4	5	6	7	8
9	10	11	12	13	14	15
16	17	18	19	20	21	22
23	24	25	26	27	28	29
30						

JULY

M	T	W	T	F	S	S
	1	2	3	4	5	6
7	8	9	10	11	12	13
14	15	16	17	18	19	20
21	22	23	24	25	26	27
28	29	30	31			

AUGUST

M	T	W	T	F	S	S
				1	2	3
4	5	6	7	8	9	10
11	12	13	14	15	16	17
18	19	20	21	22	23	24
25	26	27	28	29	30	31

SEPTEMBER

M	T	W	T	F	S	S
1	2	3	4	5	6	7
8	9	10	11	12	13	14
15	16	17	18	19	20	21
22	23	24	25	26	27	28
29	30					

OCTOBER

M	T	W	T	F	S	S
		1	2	3	4	5
6	7	8	9	10	11	12
13	14	15	16	17	18	19
20	21	22	23	24	25	26
27	28	29	30	31		

NOVEMBER

M	T	W	T	F	S	S
					1	2
3	4	5	6	7	8	9
10	11	12	13	14	15	16
17	18	19	20	21	22	23
24	25	26	27	28	29	30

DECEMBER

M	T	W	T	F	S	S
1	2	3	4	5	6	7
8	9	10	11	12	13	14
15	16	17	18	19	20	21
22	23	24	25	26	27	28
29	30	31				

JANUARY

M	T	W	T	F	S	S
			1	2	3	4
5	6	7	8	9	10	11
12	13	14	15	16	17	18
19	20	21	22	23	24	25
26	27	28	29	30	31	

FEBRUARY

M	T	W	T	F	S	S
						1
2	3	4	5	6	7	8
9	10	11	12	13	14	15
16	17	18	19	20	21	22
23	24	25	26	27	28	

MARCH

M	T	W	T	F	S	S
						1
2	3	4	5	6	7	8
9	10	11	12	13	14	15
16	17	18	19	20	21	22
23	24	25	26	27	28	29
30	31					

APRIL

M	T	W	T	F	S	S
		1	2	3	4	5
6	7	8	9	10	11	12
13	14	15	16	17	18	19
20	21	22	23	24	25	26
27	28	29	30			

MAY

M	T	W	T	F	S	S
				1	2	3
4	5	6	7	8	9	10
11	12	13	14	15	16	17
18	19	20	21	22	23	24
25	26	27	28	29	30	31

JUNE

M	T	W	T	F	S	S
1	2	3	4	5	6	7
8	9	10	11	12	13	14
15	16	17	18	19	20	21
22	23	24	25	26	27	28
29	30					

JULY

M	T	W	T	F	S	S
		1	2	3	4	5
6	7	8	9	10	11	12
13	14	15	16	17	18	19
20	21	22	23	24	25	26
27	28	29	30	31		

AUGUST

M	T	W	T	F	S	S
					1	2
3	4	5	6	7	8	9
10	11	12	13	14	15	16
17	18	19	20	21	22	23
24	25	26	27	28	29	30
31						

SEPTEMBER

M	T	W	T	F	S	S
	1	2	3	4	5	6
7	8	9	10	11	12	13
14	15	16	17	18	19	20
21	22	23	24	25	26	27
28	29	30				

OCTOBER

M	T	W	T	F	S	S
			1	2	3	4
5	6	7	8	9	10	11
12	13	14	15	16	17	18
19	20	21	22	23	24	25
26	27	28	29	30	31	

NOVEMBER

M	T	W	T	F	S	S
						1
2	3	4	5	6	7	8
9	10	11	12	13	14	15
16	17	18	19	20	21	22
23	24	25	26	27	28	29
30						

DECEMBER

M	T	W	T	F	S	S
	1	2	3	4	5	6
7	8	9	10	11	12	13
14	15	16	17	18	19	20
21	22	23	24	25	26	27
28	29	30	31			

INTRODUCTION

The illustrations reproduced in this diary come from four great nineteenth century multi-volume anthologies of rare and unusual plants from around the world.

The first to appear was Nathaniel Wallich's *Plantae Asiaticae Rariores*. Wallich (1786–1854) was Director of the Calcutta Botanic Garden, and his book was intended to depict the recently discovered plants not covered by previous illustrated works on the flora of India. The plates were printed by the new process of lithography, and the publication was fast, efficient, and better organized than any of its predecessors: it was published in three volumes, between 1829 and 1832, and Wallich proclaimed that it was "the cheapest of its kind published in any branch of natural history, every plate costing only two shillings". It contained 295 plant portraits based mostly on drawings by two Indian artists employed at the Garden, Gorachand and Vishnupersaud, and printed and coloured by John Clark. Only 250 copies were printed. Among the plants depicted was *Amherstia nobilis*, which Wallich named after Countess Amherst, and which was later to be introduced into England by John Gibson, the Duke of Devonshire's collector, and brought into flower at Chatsworth.

Only a few years later, Siebold and Zuccarini's *Flora Japonica* began to appear in Leiden. Philipp Franz von Siebold (1796–1866) was only the third European botanist to visit Japan, having officially gone there as an eye-doctor. He arrived in Japan in 1826, and was expelled four years later for the offence of trying to smuggle maps of Japan to Europe. But he managed to send a couple of consignments of Japanese plants to Europe, where he established a garden and nursery at Leiden, and helped to distribute Japanese plants to European gardens. (He eventually returned to Japan, after it was forcibly opened to western commerce in the 1850s.) The plates in the *Flora Japonica* were drawn by European artists, but in many cases were based on drawings by Japanese artists that Siebold had brought back, as not all the plants depicted were available in his garden. Most of the book was issued between 1835 and 1841, with 151 coloured plates, but a final portion was added in 1870, by F. A. W. Miquel, the Director of the Leiden Botanic Garden.

Meanwhile, a major work on the central European flora had been begun by Ludwig Reichenbach (1793–1869), the Director of the Dresden Botanic Garden. Reichenbach, who was a fine botanical artist, had already been issuing a miscellaneous collection of plant portraits entitled *Iconographia Botanica*; the second part of this (1837) doubled as the first volume of a new work entitled *Icones Florae Germanicae et Helveticae* – in effect, a flora of central Europe. Reichenbach was the author and illustrator for the first twelve volumes. In 1851 his son Gustav Heinrich Reichenbach (1823–89) took over the publication, and drew at least 1500 plates for the work. Gustav was a leading orchid expert and dealt with orchids in volumes 13–14; to make an already confusing publication history more tangled, he released these volumes as a separate work entitled *Tentamen Orchidographiae Europeae*. After his death, the work was continued by Beck von Mannagetta, and was finally completed in 1914 with its 25th volume.

Our final source for this address book is the *Icones ad floram Europae*, by Alexis Jordan and Jules Fourreau. This work began to appear in 1866, and was cut short in 1870 when Fourreau was killed in the Franco-Prussian War; Jordan's son Camille recommenced it in 1903, issuing the remaining plates that had already been made and supplying the residual text. The 501 coloured lithographic plates are splendid plant portraits, but the work is regarded with suspicion by botanists. Jordan (1814–97) became notorious for advocating a very narrow concept of species, and he distinguished as separate species many plants that everyone else regarded as minor variations. But in consequence these plates have a degree of careful detail that places them in the top rank of botanical illustrations.

Brent Elliott
The Royal Horticultural Society

December & January

2008
WEEK 1

31 Monday

New Year's Eve
Last Quarter

1 Tuesday

New Year's Day Holiday, UK, Republic of Ireland,
Canada, USA, Australia and New Zealand

2 Wednesday

Holiday, Scotland and New Zealand

3 Thursday

4 Friday

5 Saturday

6 Sunday

Epiphany

Cyclamen lobospilum [now *Cyclamen repandum*]. Hand coloured engraving after C. Delorme from Alexis Jordan & Jules Fourreau, *Icones ad floram Europae* (1866–1903).

January

2008
WEEK 2

7 Monday

8 Tuesday

New Moon

9 Wednesday

10 Thursday

Islamic New Year (subject to sighting of the moon)

11 Friday

12 Saturday

13 Sunday

Melanorrhoea usitata. Hand-coloured engraving after Gorachand from Nathaniel Wallich,
Plantae Asiaticae rariores (1829–32), believed to have been coloured by John Clark.

January

2008
WEEK 3

14 Monday

15 Tuesday

RHS London Flower Show
First Quarter

16 Wednesday

RHS London Flower Show

17 Thursday

18 Friday

19 Saturday

20 Sunday

Amherstia nobilis. Hand-coloured engraving after Vishnupersaud from Nathaniel Wallich
Plantae Asiaticae rariores (1829–32), believed to have been coloured by John Clark.

January

2008
WEEK 4

21 Monday

Holiday, USA (Martin Luther King's birthday)

22 Tuesday

Full Moon

23 Wednesday

24 Thursday

25 Friday

26 Saturday

27 Sunday

Dendrobium densiflorum. Hand-coloured engraving after Gorachand from Nathaniel Wallich,
Plantae Asiaticae rariores (1829–32), believed to have been coloured by John Clark.

January & February

2008
WEEK 5

---

28 Monday

Holiday, Australia (Australia Day)

---

29 Tuesday

---

30 Wednesday

Last Quarter

---

31 Thursday

---

1 Friday

---

2 Saturday

---

3 Sunday

Mussaenda macrophylla [now *Mussaenda frondosa*]. Hand-coloured engraving after Gorachand from Nathaniel Wallich, *Plantae Asiaticae rariores* (1829–32), believed to have been coloured by John Clark.

February

2008
WEEK 6

4 Monday

5 Tuesday

Shrove Tuesday

6 Wednesday

Ash Wednesday
Holiday, New Zealand (Waitangi Day)

7 Thursday

New Moon
Chinese New Year

8 Friday

9 Saturday

10 Sunday

Curcuma cordata [now *Curcuma petiolata*]. Unsigned hand-coloured engraving from Nathaniel Wallich, *Plantae Asiaticae rariores* (1829–32), believed to have been coloured by John Clark.

February

WEEK

---

11 Monday

---

12 Tuesday

Holiday, USA (Lincoln's Birthday)
RHS London Flower Show

---

13 Wednesday

RHS London Flower Show

---

14 Thursday

St Valentine's Day
First Quarter

---

15 Friday

---

16 Saturday

---

17 Sunday

Botryanthus compactus [now *Muscari botryoides*]. Unsigned hand-coloured engraving from Alexis Jordan & Jules Fourreau, *Icones ad floram Europae* (1866–1903).

February

2008
WEEK 8

18 Monday

Holiday, USA (Washington's Birthday)

19 Tuesday

20 Wednesday

21 Thursday

Full Moon

22 Friday

23 Saturday

24 Sunday

Narcissus jonquilla, Narcissus dubius, Narcissus tazetta. Unsigned hand-coloured engraving from H. G. L. Reichenbach et al., *Icones florae Germanicae et Helveticae*, vol. 9 (1847).

February & March

WEEK

25 Monday

26 Tuesday

27 Wednesday

28 Thursday

29 Friday

Last Quarter

1 Saturday

St David's Day

2 Sunday

Mothering Sunday, UK

Gentiana angustifolia. Hand-coloured engraving after H. G. Reichenbach from
H. G. L. Reichenbach et al., *Icones florae Germanicae et Helveticae*, vol. 17 (1854–55).

March

2008
WEEK 10

3 Monday

4 Tuesday

5 Wednesday

6 Thursday

7 Friday

New Moon

8 Saturday

9 Sunday

Camellia japonica. Unsigned hand-coloured engraving from Philipp Franz von Siebold & J. G. Zuccarini, *Flora Japonica* (1835–41).

March

2008
WEEK 11

10 Monday

Commonwealth Day

11 Tuesday

RHS London Flower Show

12 Wednesday

RHS London Flower Show

13 Thursday

14 Friday

First Quarter

15 Saturday

RHS London Orchid Show

16 Sunday

Palm Sunday
RHS London Orchid Show

Primula x pubescens. Hand-coloured engraving after Humnitz [?] from H. G. L. Reichenbach et al., *Icones florae Germanicae et Helveticae*, vol. 17 (1854–55).

March

2008
WEEK 12

17 Monday

St Patrick's Day
Holiday, Northern Ireland and Republic of Ireland

18 Tuesday

19 Wednesday

20 Thursday

Maundy Thursday
Vernal Equinox

21 Friday

Good Friday
Holiday, UK, Canada, USA,
Australia and New Zealand
Full Moon

22 Saturday

23 Sunday

Easter Sunday

Ajax gayi [now *Narcissus pseudonarcissus* cv., probably *N. pseudonarcissus* 'Princeps'.]. Hand-coloured engraving after C. Delorme from Alexis Jordan & Jules Fourreau, *Icones ad floram Europae* (1866–1903).

March

2008
WEEK 13

---

24 Monday

Easter Monday Holiday, UK (exc. Scotland), Republic of Ireland, Canada, Australia and New Zealand

---

25 Tuesday

---

26 Wednesday

---

27 Thursday

---

28 Friday

---

29 Saturday

Last Quarter

---

30 Sunday

British Summertime begins

Aeschynanthus parviflorus. Hand-coloured engraving after Gorachand from Nathaniel Wallich, *Plantae Asiaticae rariores* (1829–32), believed to have been coloured by John Clark.

March & April

2008
WEEK 14

31 Monday

1 Tuesday

2 Wednesday

3 Thursday

4 Friday

5 Saturday

6 Sunday

New Moon

Erythronium dens-canis. Unsigned hand-coloured engraving from H. G. L. Reichenbach et al., *Icones florae Germanicae et Helveticae*, vol. 10 (1848).

April

2008
WEEK

7 Monday

8 Tuesday

9 Wednesday

10 Thursday

11 Friday

12 Saturday

First Quarter

13 Sunday

Rhododendron formosum. Hand-coloured engraving after Gorachand from Nathaniel Wallich, *Plantae Asiaticae rariores* (1829–32), believed to have been coloured by John Clark.

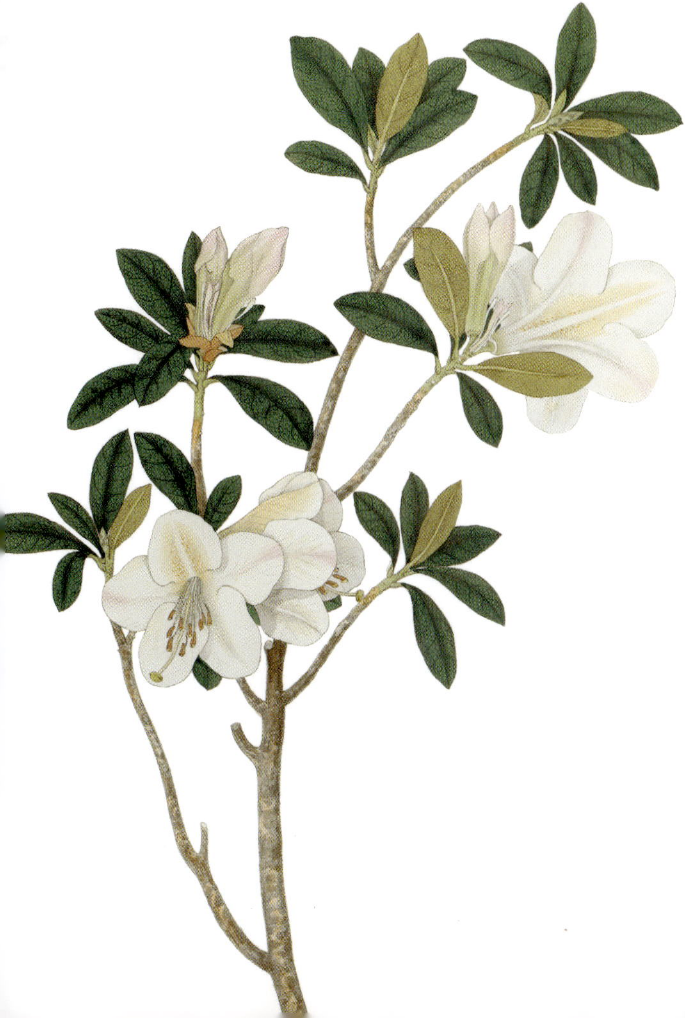

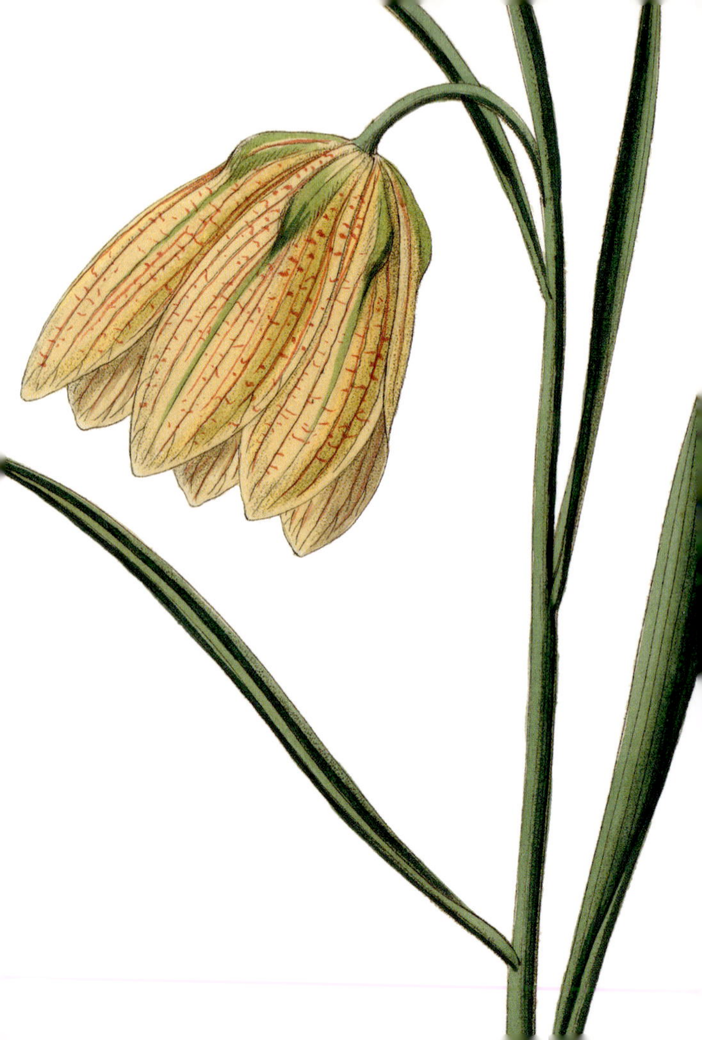

April

2008
WEEK 16

14 Monday

15 Tuesday

RHS London Flower Show

16 Wednesday

RHS London Flower Show

17 Thursday

18 Friday

RHS Spring Flower Show, Cardiff (to be confirmed)

19 Saturday

RHS Spring Flower Show, Cardiff (to be confirmed)

20 Sunday

Passover (Pesach), First Day
RHS Spring Flower Show, Cardiff (to be confirmed)
Full Moon

Fritillaria lutea. Unsigned hand-coloured engraving from H. G. L. Reichenbach et al.,
Icones florae Germanicae et Helveticae, vol. 10 (1848).

April

2008
WEEK 1

---
21 Monday

Birthday of Queen Elizabeth II

---
22 Tuesday

---
23 Wednesday

St George's Day

---
24 Thursday

---
25 Friday

Holiday, Australia and New Zealand (Anzac Day)

---
26 Saturday

Passover (Pesach), Seventh Day

---
27 Sunday

Passover (Pesach), Eighth Day

Magnolia insignis. Hand-coloured engraving after Vishnupersaud from Nathaniel Wallich, *Plantae Asiaticae rariores* (1829–32), believed to have been coloured by John Clark.

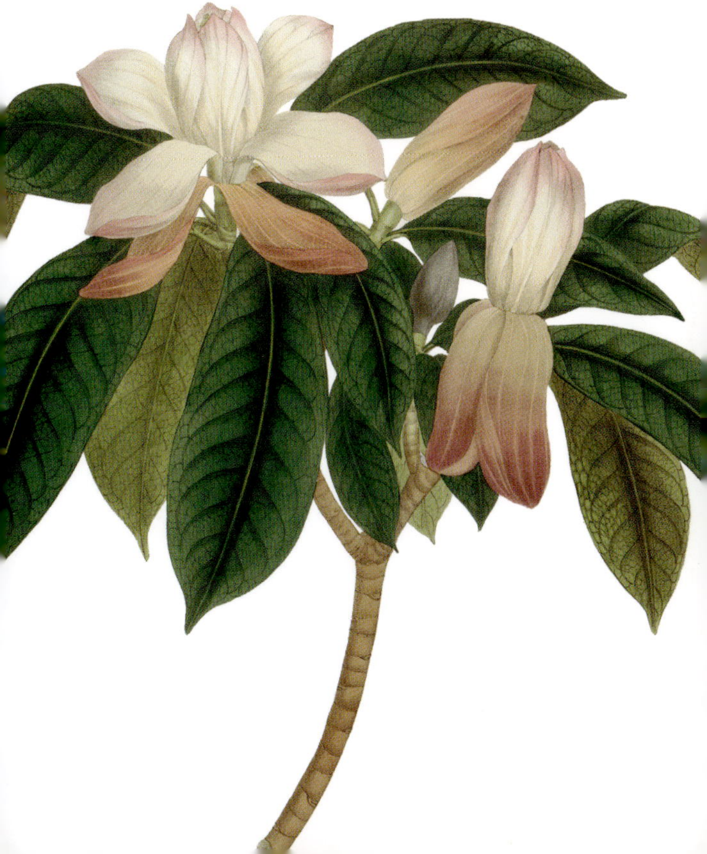

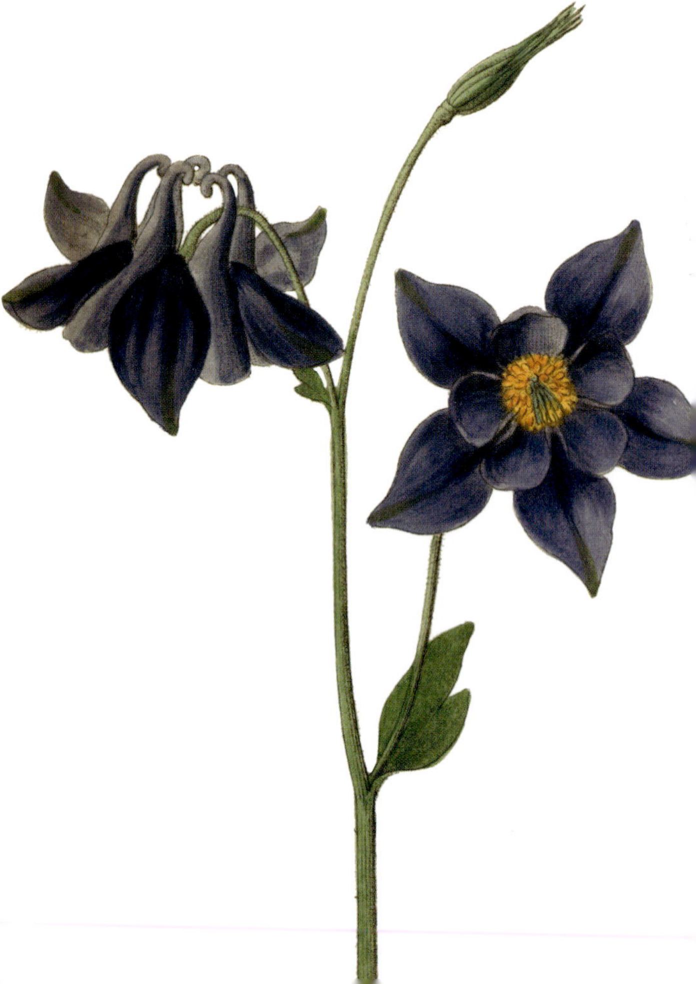

April & May

2008
WEEK 18

28 Monday

Last Quarter

29 Tuesday

RHS Late Daffodil Competition, Wisley

30 Wednesday

RHS Late Daffodil Competition, Wisley

1 Thursday

Ascension Day

2 Friday

3 Saturday

4 Sunday

Aquilegia vulgaris. Unsigned hand-coloured engraving from H. G. L. Reichenbach et al., *Icones florae Germanicae et Helveticae*, vol. 4 (1840).

May

2008
WEEK 19

---
5 Monday

Early May Bank Holiday, UK and Republic of Ireland
New Moon

---
6 Tuesday

---
7 Wednesday

---
8 Thursday

Malvern Spring Gardening Show

---
9 Friday

Malvern Spring Gardening Show

---
10 Saturday

Malvern Spring Gardening Show

---
11 Sunday

Whit Sunday (Pentecost)
Mother's Day, Canada, USA, Australia and New Zealand
Malvern Spring Gardening Show

Tulipa platystigma [now *Tulipa gesneriana*]. Hand-coloured engraving after A. Mignol from Alexis Jordan & Jules Fourreau, *Icones ad floram Europae* (1866–1903).

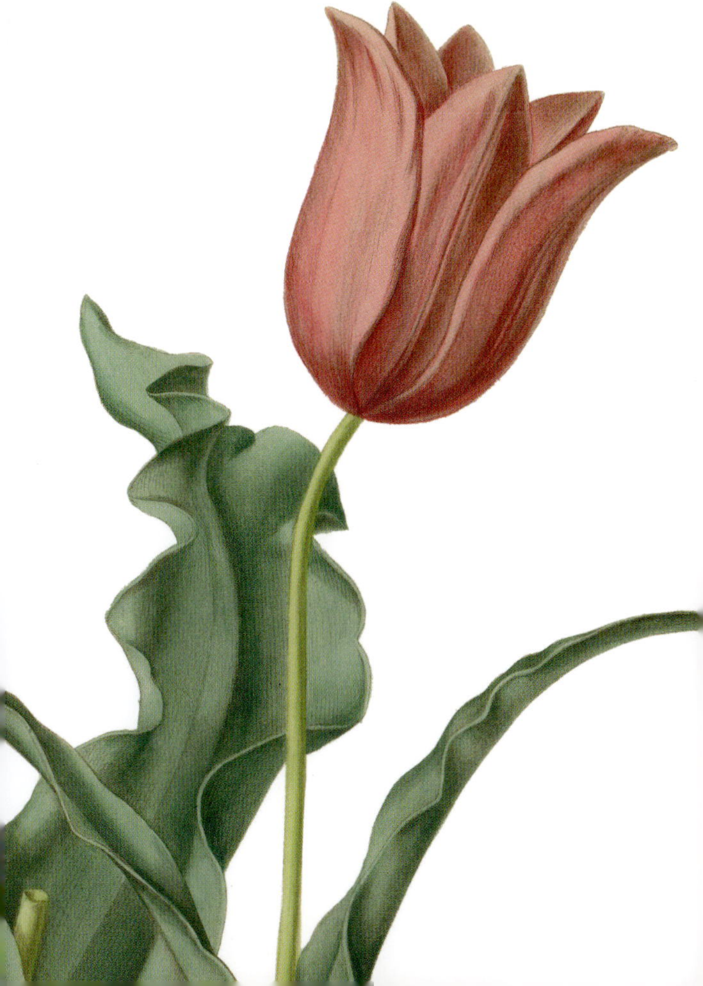

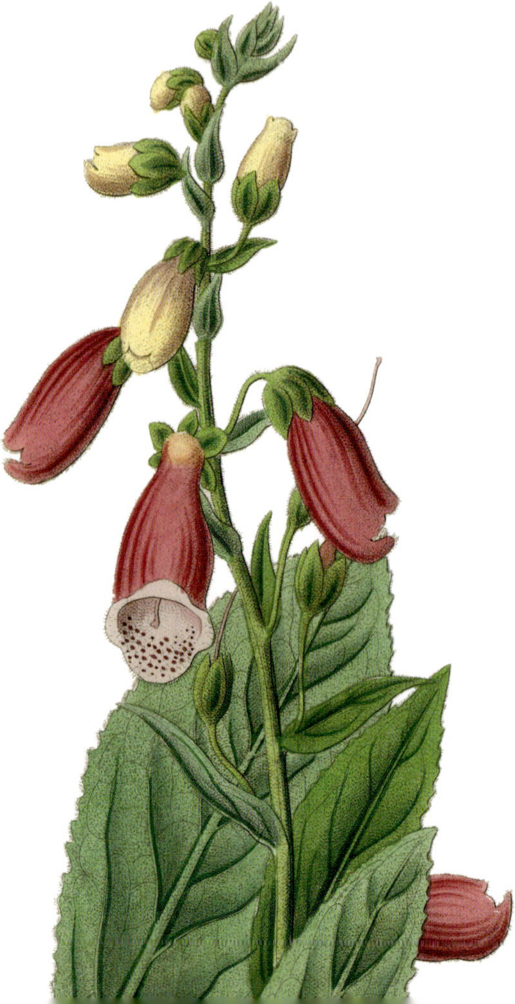

May

2008
WEEK 20

12 Monday

First Quarter

13 Tuesday

14 Wednesday

15 Thursday

16 Friday

17 Saturday

18 Sunday

Trinity Sunday

Digitalis thapsi. Hand-coloured engraving after H. G. Reichenbach from H. G. L. Reichenbach et al., *Icones florae Germanicae et Helveticae*, vol. 20 (1861).

May

2008
WEEK 21

19 Monday

Holiday, Canada (Victoria Day)

20 Tuesday

Chelsea Flower Show
Full Moon

21 Wednesday

Chelsea Flower Show

22 Thursday

Corpus Christi
Chelsea Flower Show

23 Friday

Chelsea Flower Show

24 Saturday

Chelsea Flower Show

25 Sunday

Campanula latifolia 'Eriocarpa' [now absorbed into *Campanula latifolia*]. Hand-coloured engraving after H. G. Reichenbach from H. G. L. Reichenbach et al., *Icones florae Germanicae et Helveticae*, vol. 19 (1858–60).

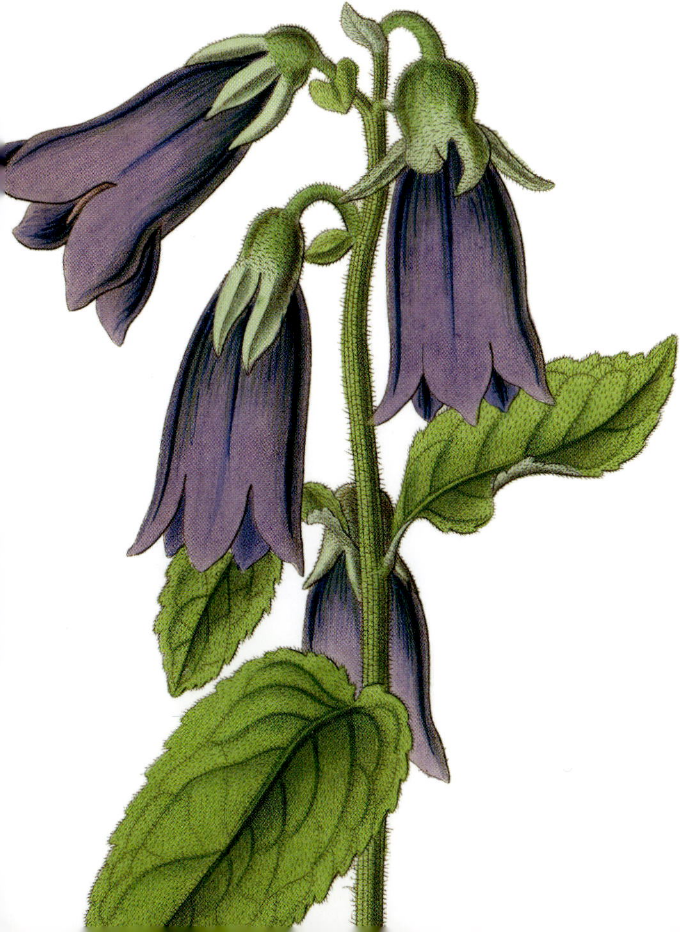

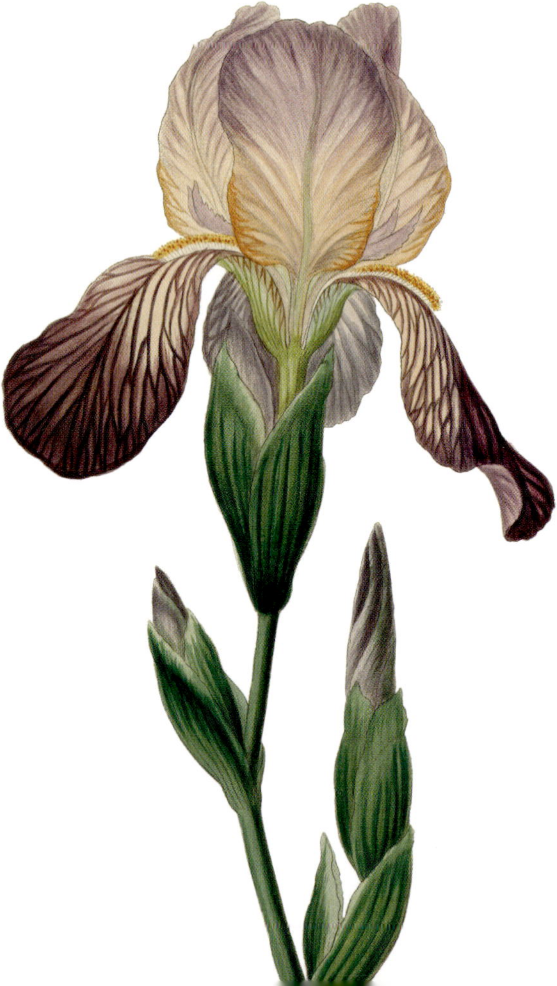

May & June

2008
WEEK 22

26 Monday

Spring Bank Holiday, UK
Holiday, USA (Memorial Day)

27 Tuesday

28 Wednesday

Last Quarter

29 Thursday

30 Friday

31 Saturday

1 Sunday

Iris x lurida. Hand-coloured engraving after Humnitz [?] from H. G. L. Reichenbach et al.,
Icones florae Germanicae et Helveticae, vol. 9 (1847).

June

2008
WEEK 23

2 Monday

Holiday, Republic of Ireland
Holiday, New Zealand (The Queen's birthday)

3 Tuesday

New Moon

4 Wednesday

5 Thursday

6 Friday

7 Saturday

8 Sunday

Paeonia peregrina. Unsigned hand-coloured engraving from H. G. L. Reichenbach et al., *Icones florae Germanicae et Helveticae,* vol. 4 (1840).

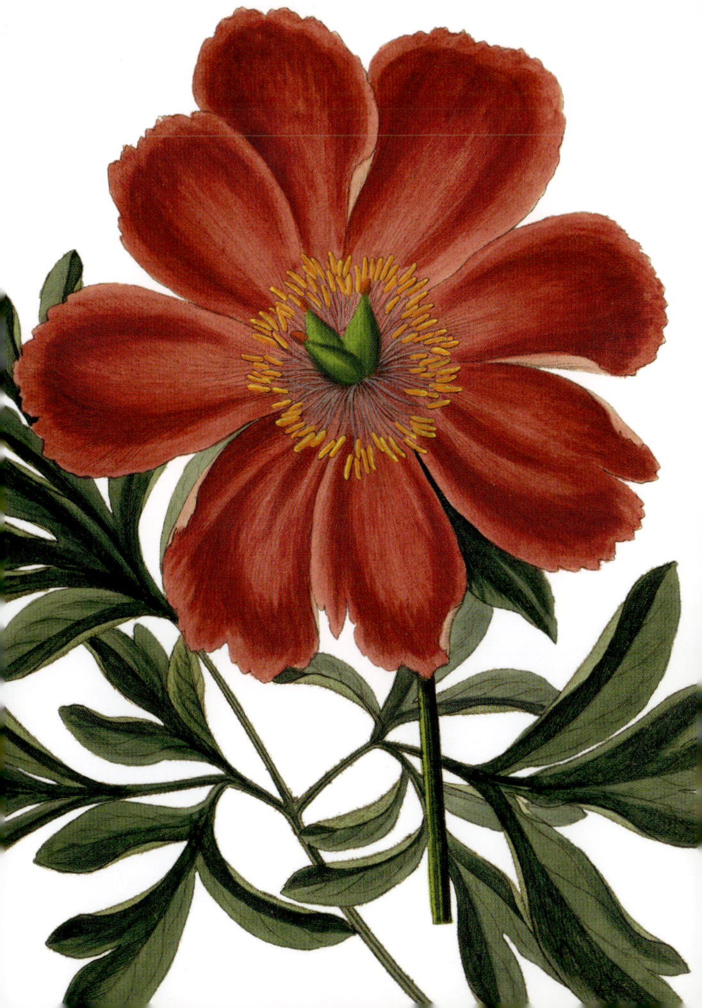

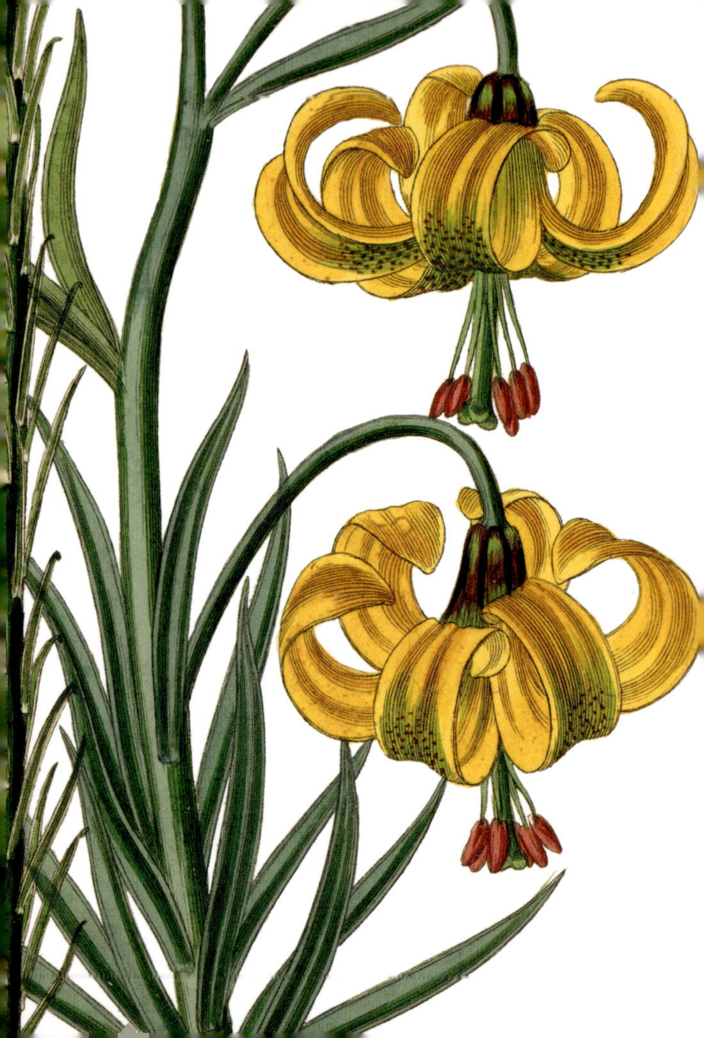

June

2008
WEEK 24

9 Monday

Jewish Feasts of Weeks (Shavuot)

10 Tuesday

First Quarter

11 Wednesday

BBC Gardeners' World Live, Birmingham

12 Thursday

BBC Gardeners' World Live, Birmingham

13 Friday

BBC Gardeners' World Live, Birmingham

14 Saturday

The Queen's official birthday (subject to confirmation)
BBC Gardeners' World Live, Birmingham

15 Sunday

Father's Day, UK, Canada and USA
BBC Gardeners' World Live, Birmingham

Lilium pyrenaicum. Unsigned hand-coloured engraving from H. G. L. Reichenbach et al., *Icones florae Germanicae et Helveticae*, vol. 10 (1848).

June

2008
WEEK 25

16 Monday

17 Tuesday

18 Wednesday

Full Moon

19 Thursday

20 Friday

Summer Solstice

21 Saturday

22 Sunday

Identification uncertain due to lack of botanical detail shown but one of the *Delphinium* species. Unsigned hand-coloured engraving from H. G. L. Reichenbach et al., *Icones florae Germanicae et Helveticae*, vol. 4 (1840).

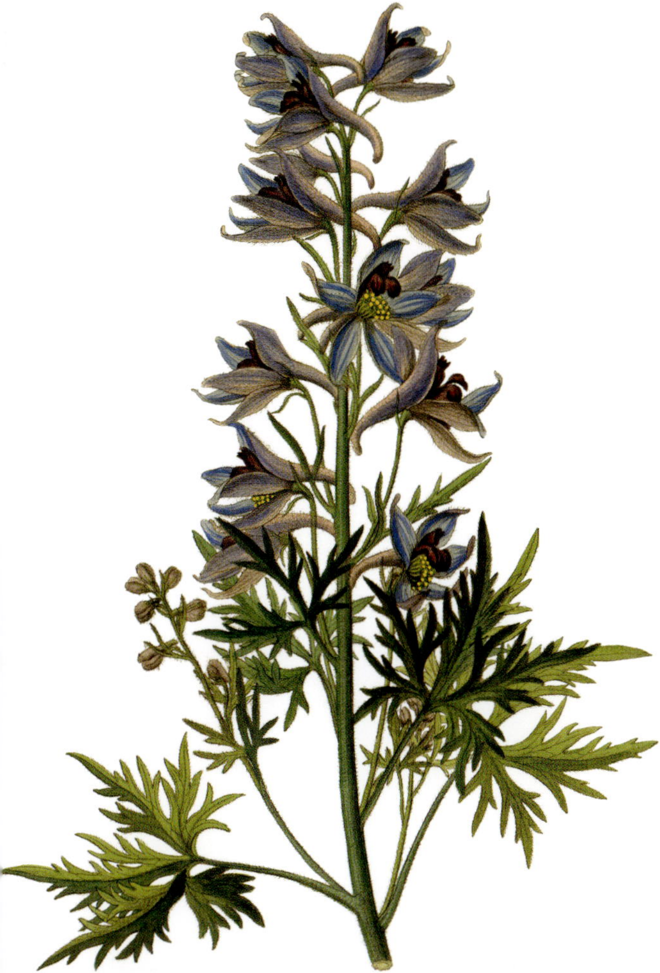

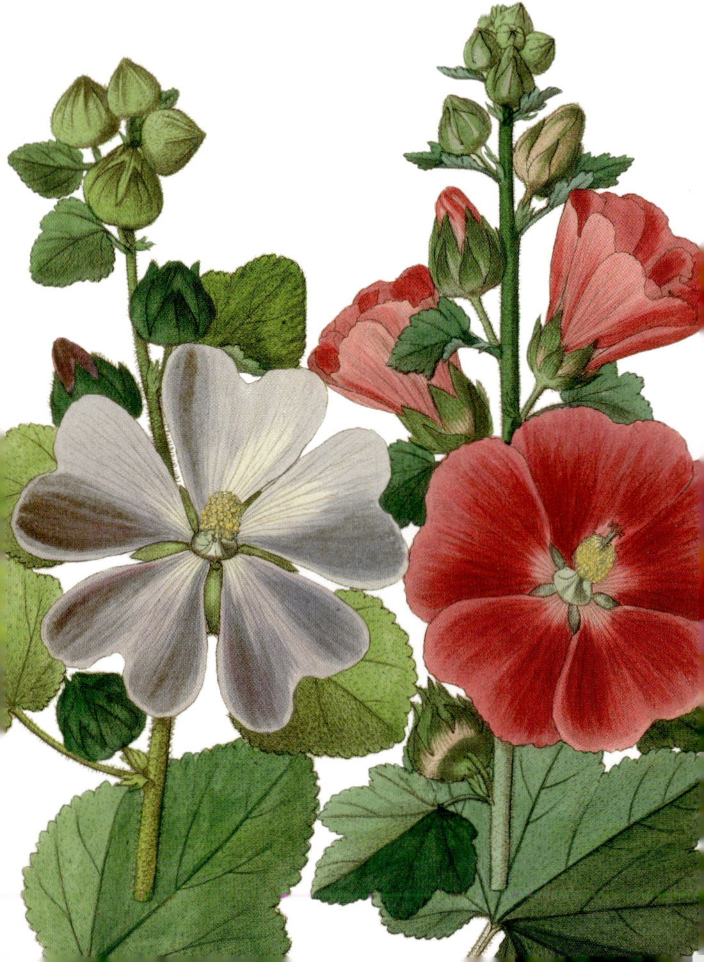

June

2008
WEEK 26

23 Monday

24 Tuesday

25 Wednesday

26 Thursday

Last Quarter

27 Friday

28 Saturday

29 Sunday

Althaea [Alcea] pallida, Alcea rosea. Unsigned hand-coloured engraving from H. G. L. Reichenbach et al., *Icones florae Germanicae et Helveticae*, vol. 5 (1841–42).

June & July

2008

30 Monday

1 Tuesday

Holiday, Canada (Canada Day)

2 Wednesday

3 Thursday

New Moon

4 Friday

Holiday, USA (Independence Day)

5 Saturday

6 Sunday

Rosa ragosa. Hand-coloured engraving after S. Minsinger from Philipp Franz von Siebold & J. G. Zuccarini, *Flora Japonica* (1835–41).

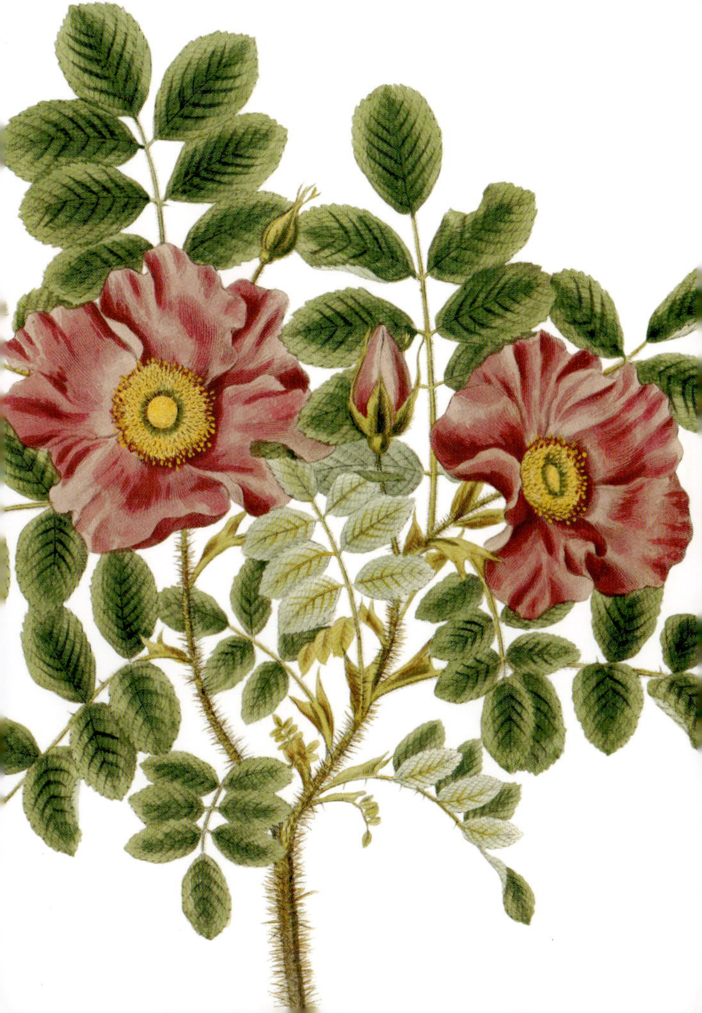

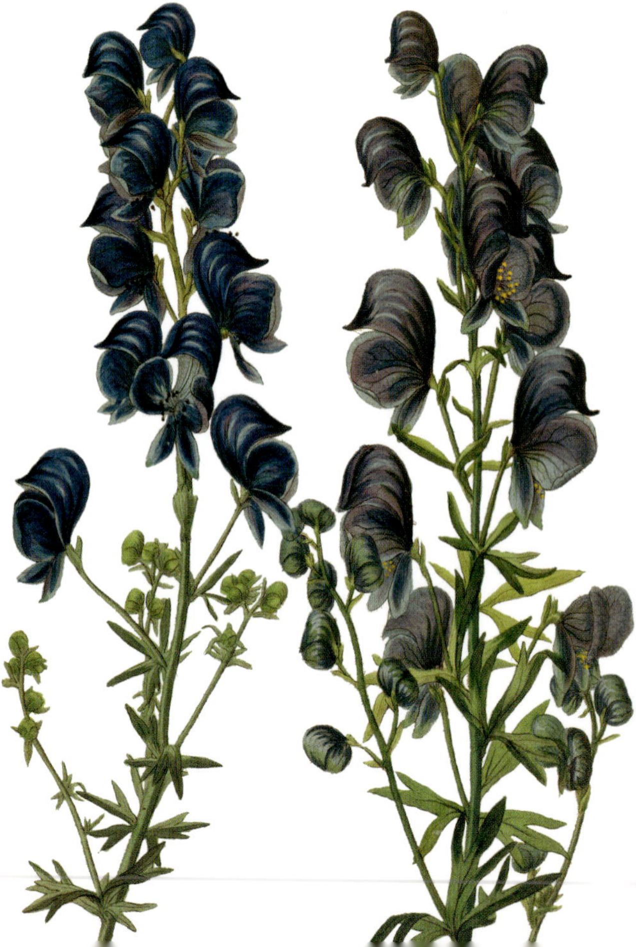

July

2008
WEEK 28

7 Monday

8 Tuesday

Hampton Court Palace Flower Show
9 Wednesday

Hampton Court Palace Flower Show
10 Thursday

Hampton Court Palace Flower Show
First Quarter
11 Friday

Hampton Court Palace Flower Show
12 Saturday

Hampton Court Palace Flower Show
13 Sunday

Hampton Court Palace Flower Show

Aconitum eminens [now *Aconitum napellus*], *Aconitum pyramidale* [now *Aconitum napellus*]. Unsigned hand-coloured engraving from H. G. L. Reichenbach et al., *Icones florae Germanicae et Helveticae*, vol. 4 (1840).

July

2008
WEEK

---

14 Monday

Holiday, Northern Ireland (Battle of the Boyne)

---

15 Tuesday

St Swithin's Day

---

16 Wednesday

---

17 Thursday

---

18 Friday

Full Moon

---

19 Saturday

---

20 Sunday

Hemerocallis flava [now *Hemerocallis lilioasphodelus*]. Unsigned hand-coloured engraving from H. G. L. Reichenbach et al., *Icones florae Germanicae et Helveticae*, vol. 10 (1848).

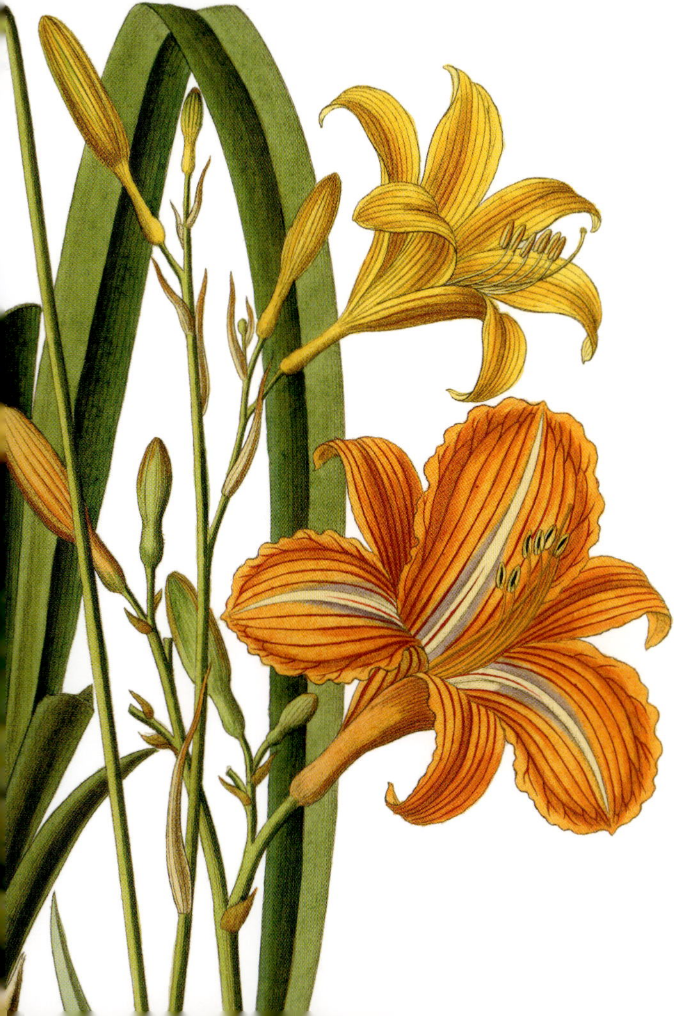

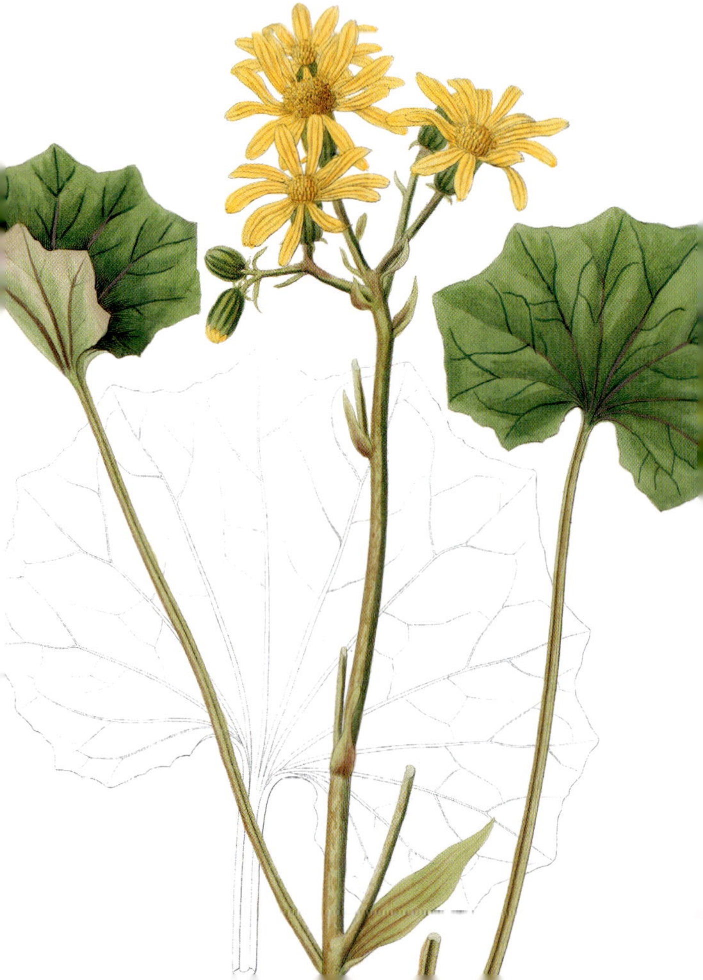

July

2008
WEEK 30

21 Monday

22 Tuesday

23 Wednesday

The RHS Flower Show at Tatton Park

24 Thursday

The RHS Flower Show at Tatton Park

25 Friday

The RHS Flower Show at Tatton Park
Last Quarter

26 Saturday

The RHS Flower Show at Tatton Park

27 Sunday

The RHS Flower Show at Tatton Park

Ligularia kaempferi [now *Farfugium japonicum*]. Hand-coloured engraving after S. Minsinger from Philipp Franz von Siebold & J. G. Zuccarini, *Flora Japonica* (1835–41).

July & August

2008
WEEK 31

28 Monday

29 Tuesday

30 Wednesday

31 Thursday

1 Friday

New Moon

2 Saturday

3 Sunday

Probably *Vinca herbacea* but identification uncertain due to lack of botanical detail shown. Hand-coloured engraving after H. G. Reichenbach from H. G. L. Reichenbach et al., *Icones florae Germanicae et Helveticae*, vol. 17 (1854–55).

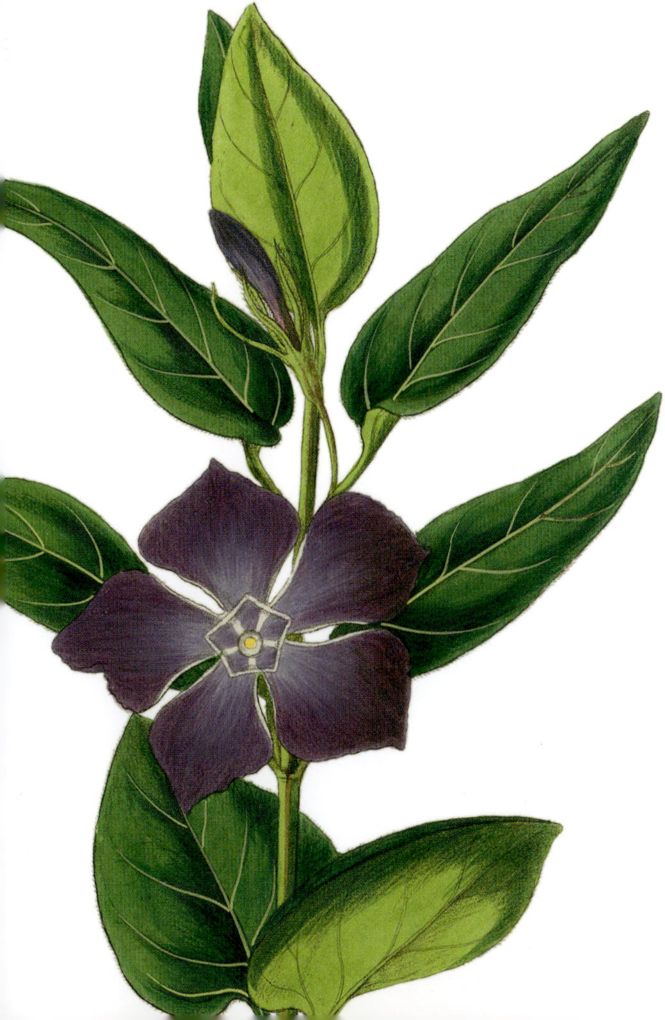

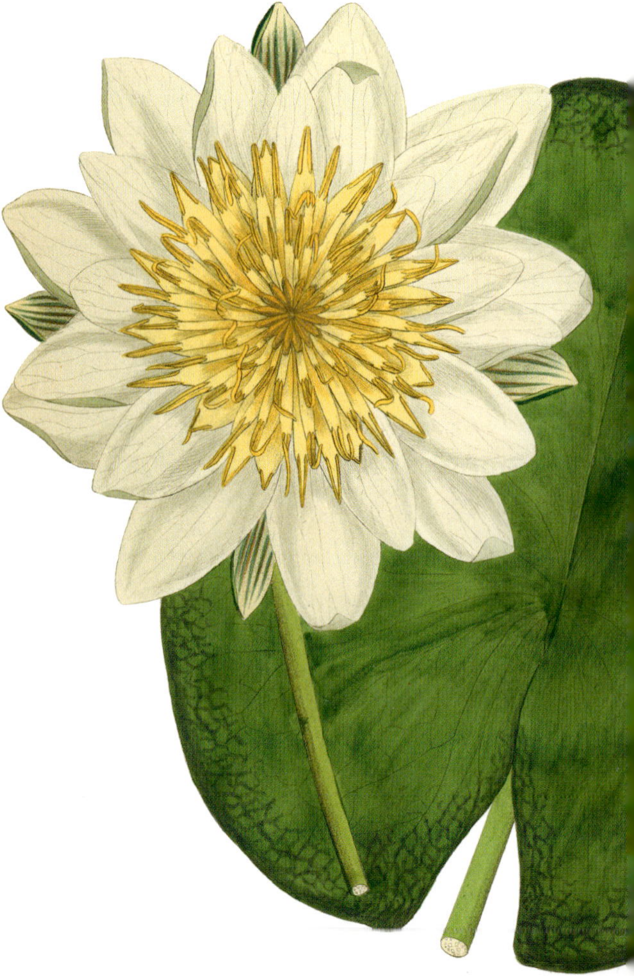

August

2008
WEEK 32

4 Monday

Summer Bank Holiday, Scotland and Republic of Ireland

5 Tuesday

6 Wednesday

7 Thursday

8 Friday

First Quarter

9 Saturday

10 Sunday

Nymphaea alba. Unsigned hand-coloured engraving from H. G. L. Reichenbach et al., *Icones florae Germanicae et Helveticae*, vol. 7 (1845).

August

2008
WEEK 33

11 Monday

12 Tuesday

13 Wednesday

14 Thursday

15 Friday

16 Saturday

Full Moon

17 Sunday

Nerium oleander. Hand-coloured engraving after H. G. Reichenbach from H. G. L. Reichenbach et al., *Icones florae Germanicae et Helveticae*, vol. 17 (1854–55).

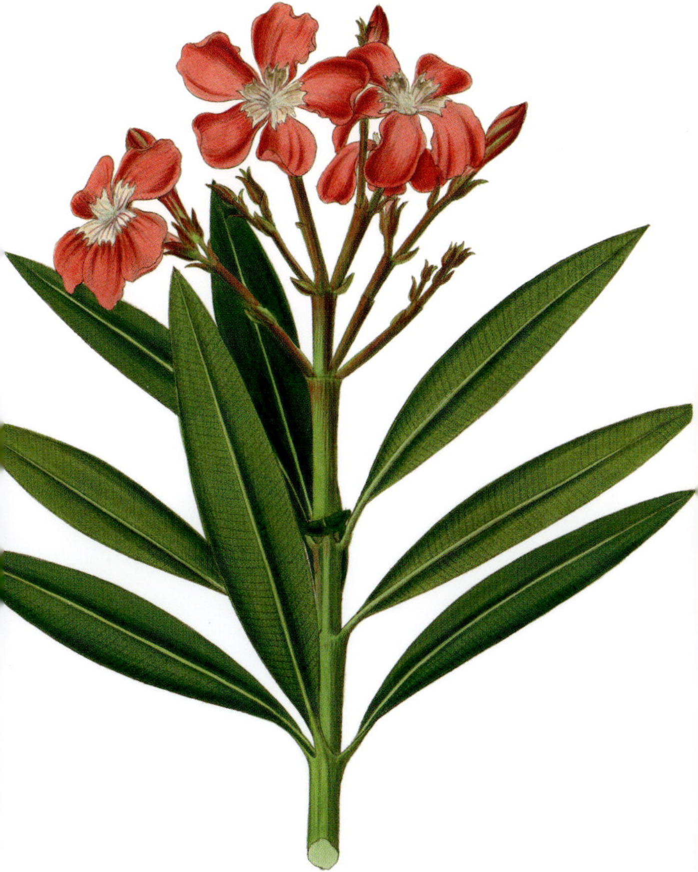

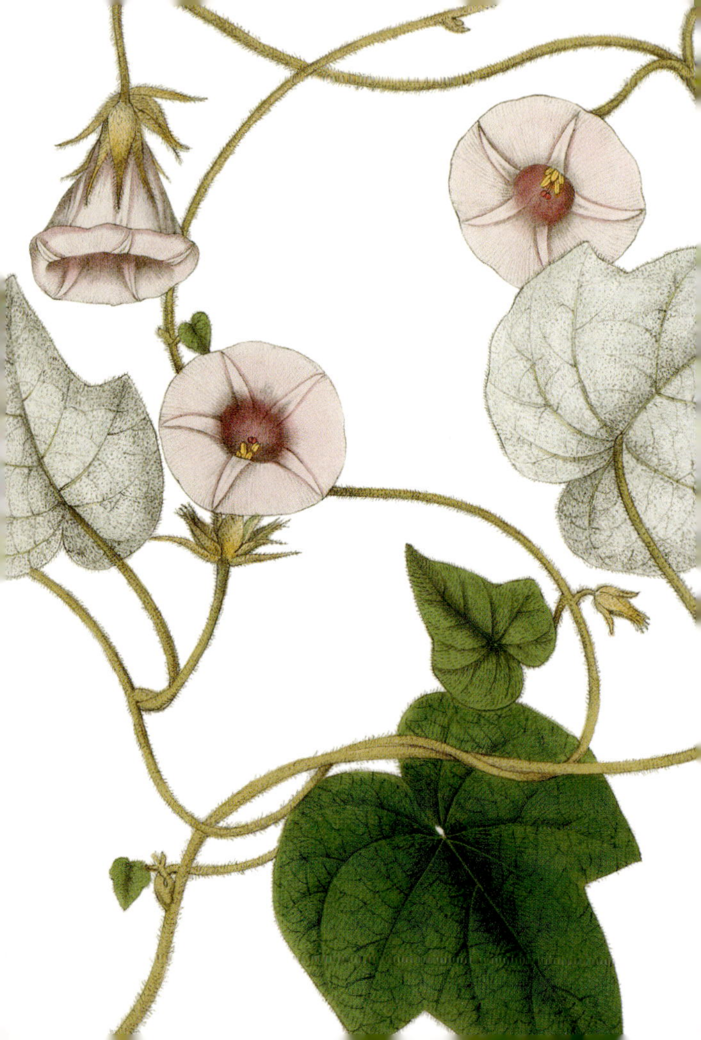

August

2008
WEEK 34

18 Monday

19 Tuesday

Wisley Flower Show

20 Wednesday

Wisley Flower Show

21 Thursday

Wisley Flower Show

22 Friday

23 Saturday

Last Quarter

24 Sunday

Convolvulus wightii [now *Ipomoea wightii*]. Hand-coloured engraving after Vishnupersaud from Nathaniel Wallich, *Plantae Asiaticae rariores* (1829–32), believed to have been coloured by John Clark.

August

2008
WEEK 3

25 Monday

Summer Bank Holiday, UK (exc. Scotland)

26 Tuesday

27 Wednesday

28 Thursday

29 Friday

30 Saturday

New Moon

31 Sunday

Eryngium maritimum. Hand-coloured engraving after H. G. Reichenbach from H. G. L. Reichenbach et al., *Icones florae Germanicae et Helveticae*, vol. 21 (1863).

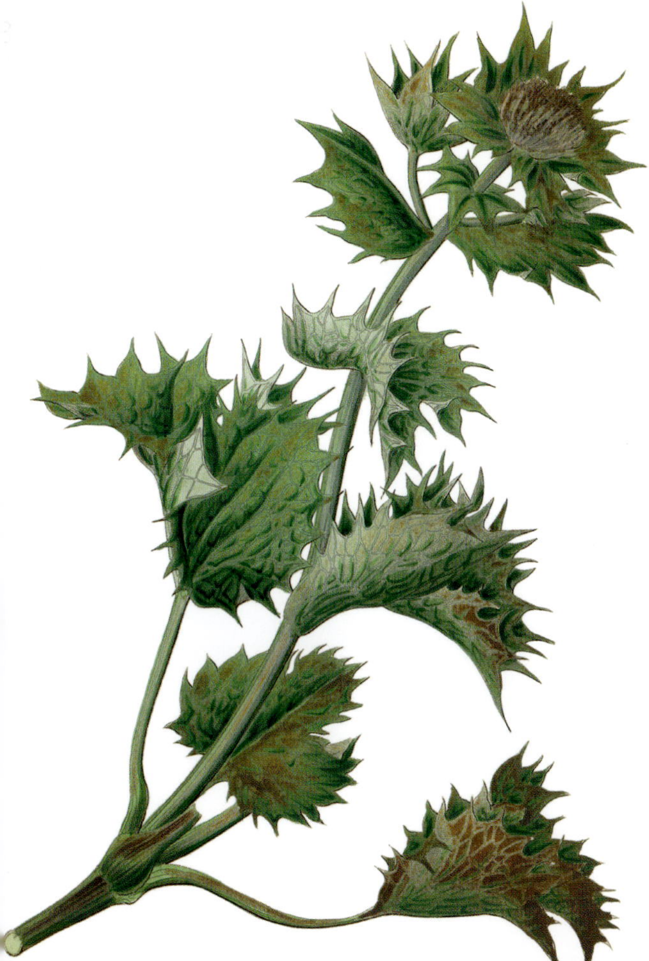

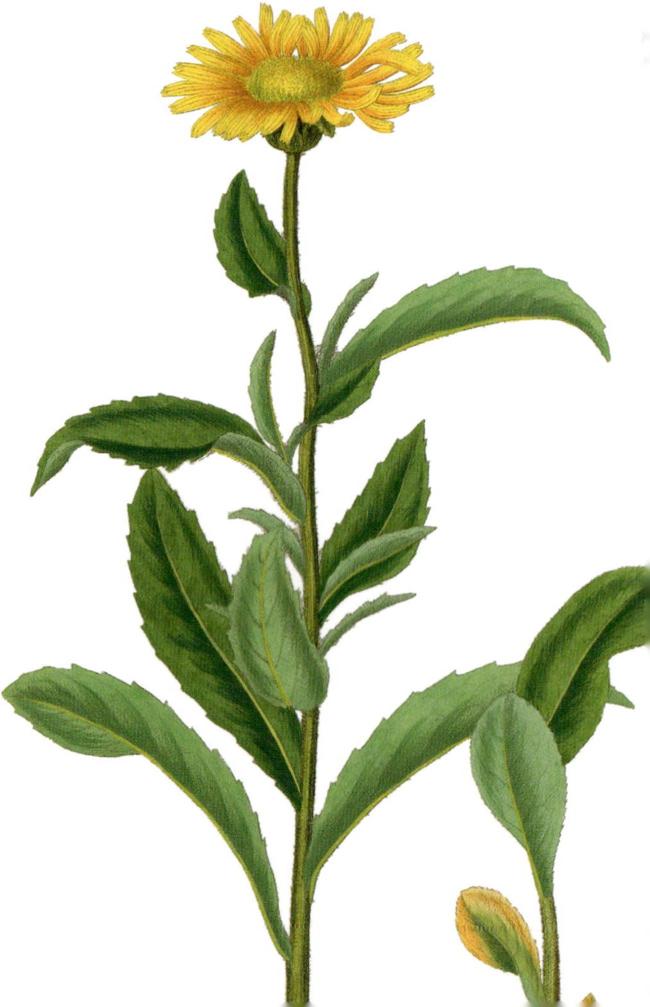

September

2008
WEEK 36

1 Monday

Holiday, Canada (Labour Day) and USA (Labor Day)

2 Tuesday

First Day of Ramadan (subject to sighting of the moon)

3 Wednesday

4 Thursday

5 Friday

6 Saturday

7 Sunday

Father's Day, Australia and New Zealand
First Quarter

Inula hirta. Hand-coloured engraving after H. G. Reichenbach from H. G. L. Reichenbach et al., *Icones florae Germanicae et Helveticae*, vol. 16 (1853–54).

September

2008
WEEK 37

---

8 Monday

---

9 Tuesday

---

10 Wednesday

---

11 Thursday

---

12 Friday

---

13 Saturday

---

14 Sunday

Hibiscus hamabo. Unsigned hand-coloured engraving from Philipp Franz von Siebold & J. G. Zuccarini, *Flora Japonica* (1835–41).

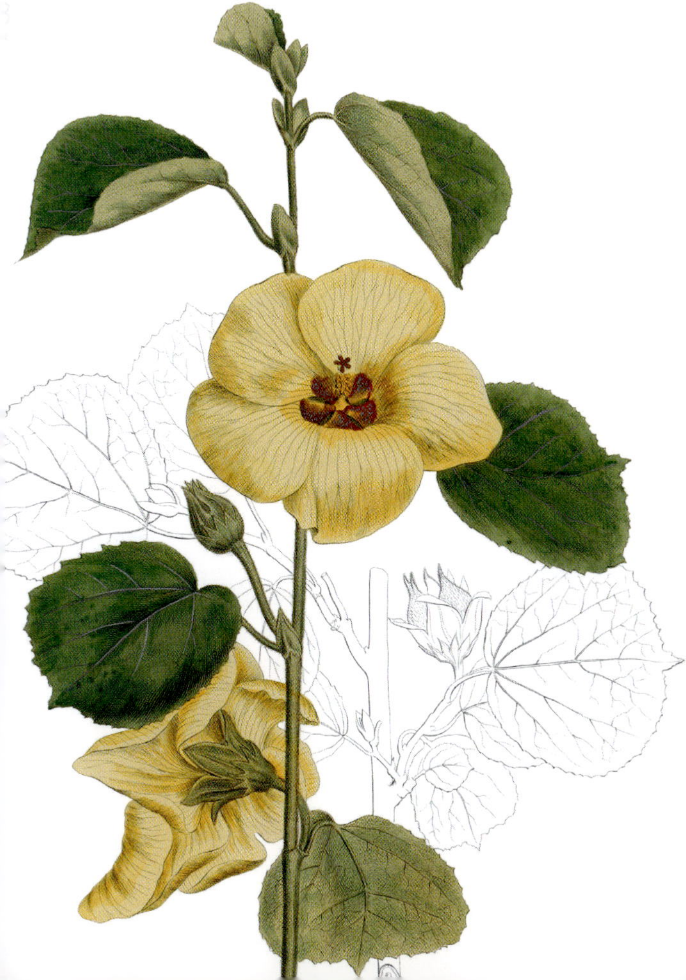

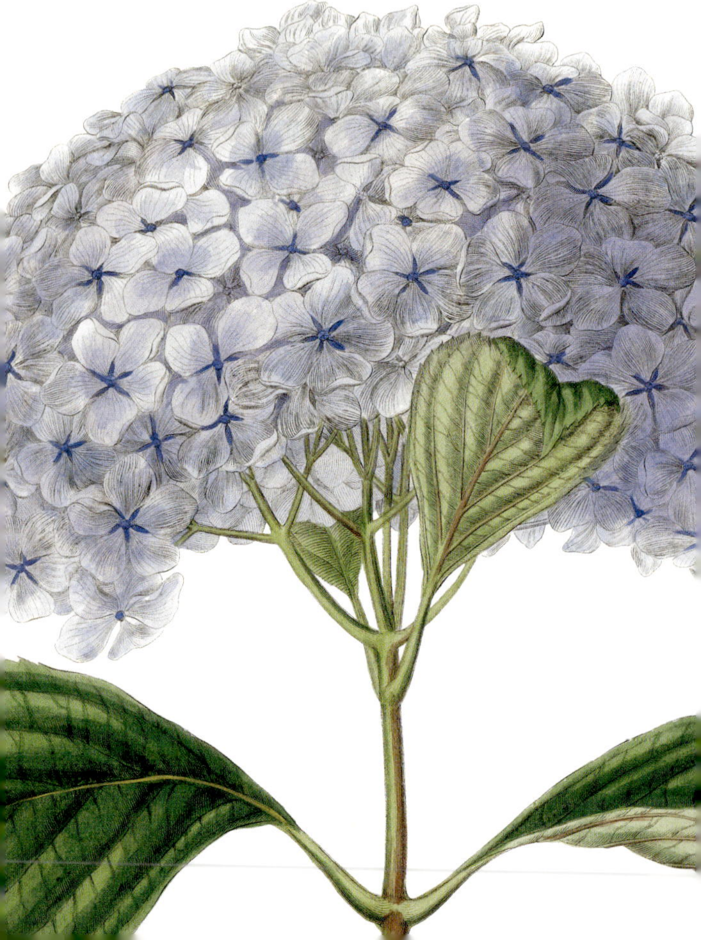

September

2008
WEEK 38

15 Monday

Full Moon

16 Tuesday

RHS London Late Summer Show

17 Wednesday

RHS London Late Summer Show

18 Thursday

19 Friday

20 Saturday

21 Sunday

Hydrangea otaksa [now *Hydrangea macrophylla* 'Otaksa']. Hand-coloured engraving after S. Minsinger from Philipp Franz von Siebold & J. G. Zuccarini, *Flora Japonica* (1835–41).

September

2008
WEEK 00

22 Monday

Autumnal Equinox
Last Quarter

23 Tuesday

24 Wednesday

25 Thursday

26 Friday

27 Saturday

Malvern Autumn Show

28 Sunday

Malvern Autumn Show

Lathyrus heterophyllus. Hand-coloured engraving after Humnitz [?] from
H. G. L Reichenbach, *Icones florae Germanicae*, vol. 22 (1867).

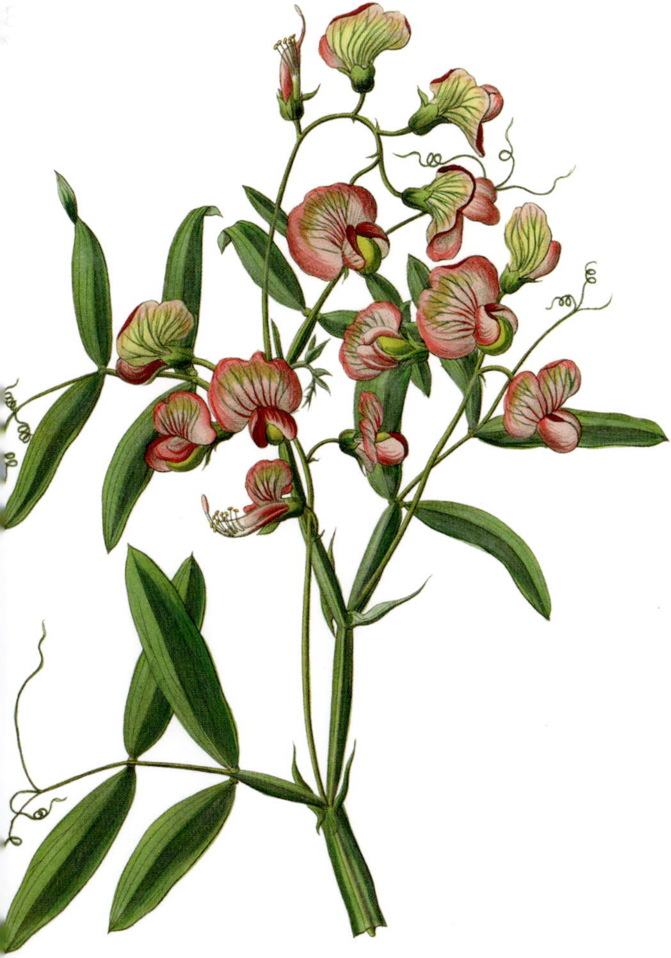

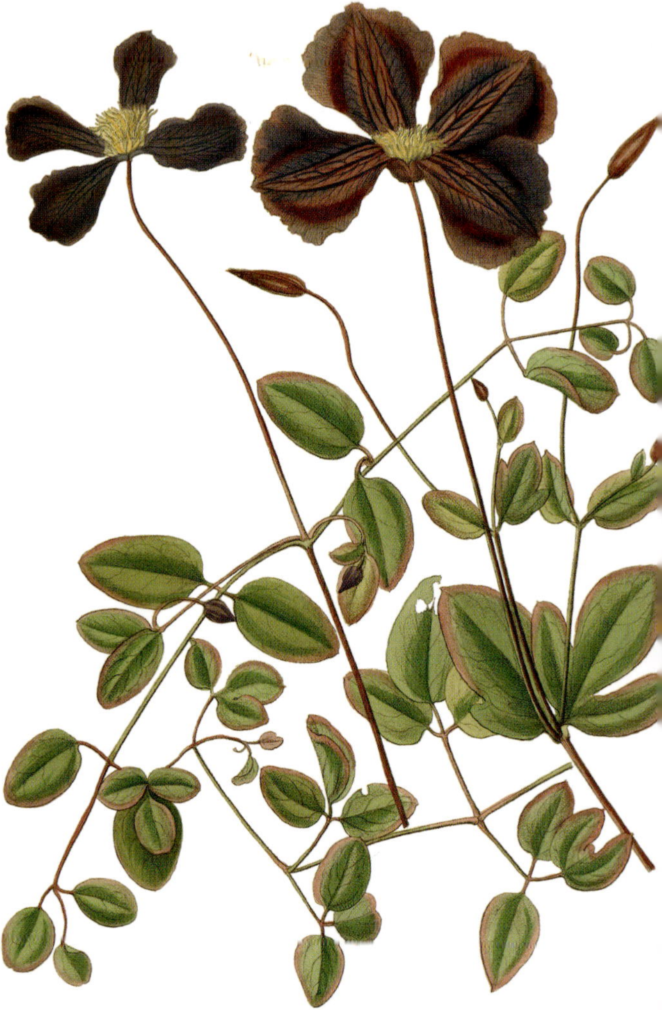

September&October

2008
WEEK 40

29 Monday

Michaelmas Day
New Moon

30 Tuesday

Jewish New Year (Rosh Hashanah)

1 Wednesday

2 Thursday

3 Friday

4 Saturday

5 Sunday

Clematis viticella. Unsigned hand-coloured engraving from H. G. L. Reichenbach et al., *Icones florae Germanicae et Helveticae*, vol. 4 (1840).

October

2008
WEEK 41

6 Monday

---

7 Tuesday

RHS London Great Autumn Show
First Quarter

---

8 Wednesday

RHS London Great Autumn Show

9 Thursday

Jewish Day of Atonement (Yom Kippur)

10 Friday

---

11 Saturday

---

12 Sunday

Eriophorum scheuchzeri. Unsigned hand-coloured engraving from H. G. L. Reichenbach et al., *Icones florae Germanicae et Helveticae*, vol. 8 (1846).

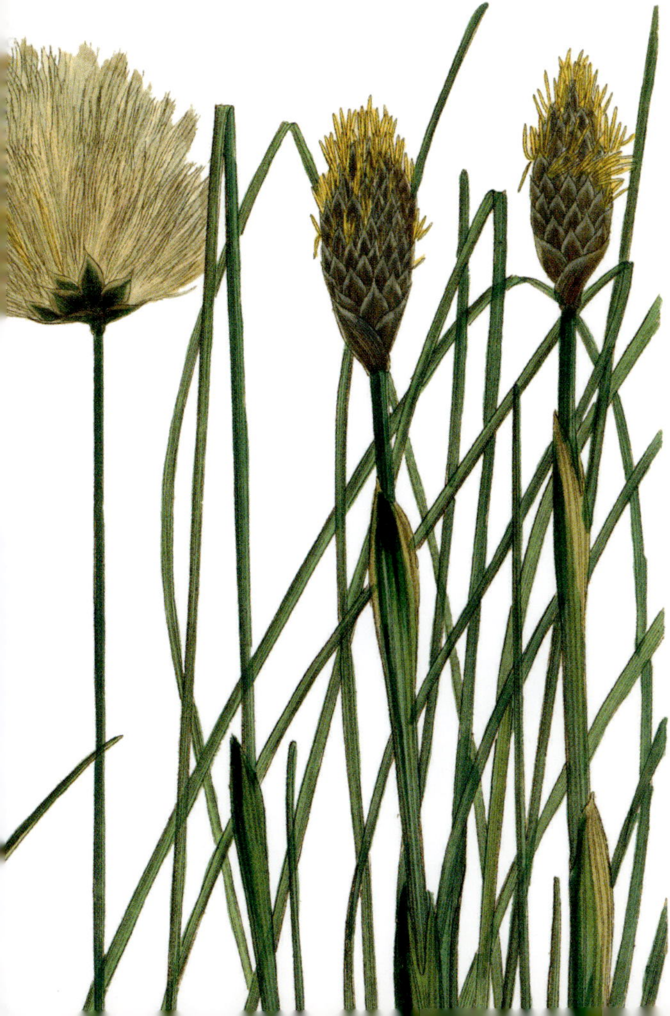

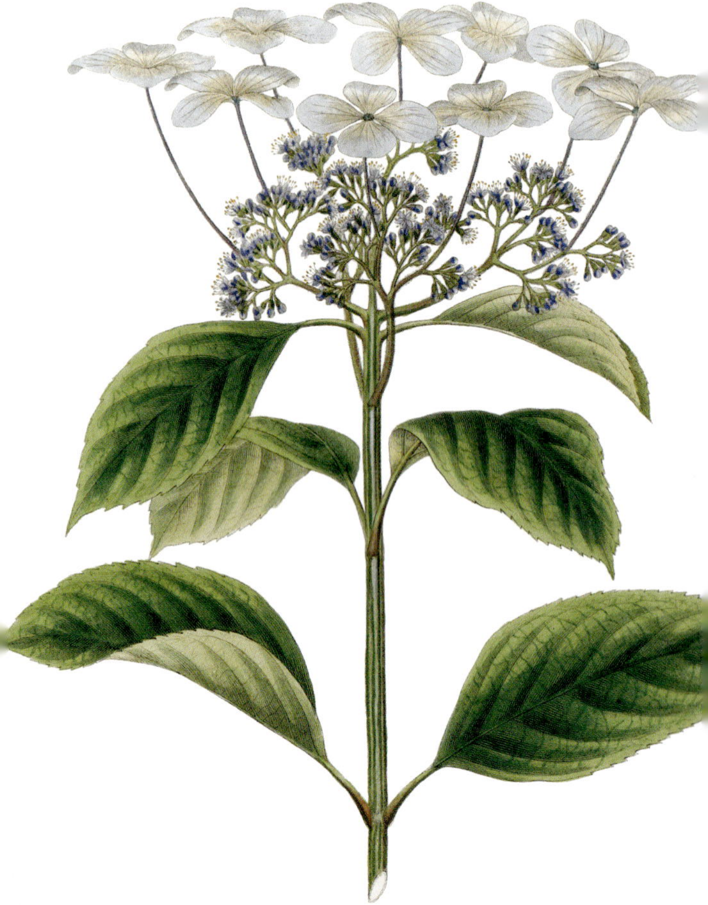

October

2008
WEEK 42

13 Monday

Holiday, Canada, (Thanksgiving Day)
Holiday, USA (Columbus Day)

14 Tuesday

Jewish Festival Tabernacles (Succoth), First Day
Full Moon

15 Wednesday

16 Thursday

17 Friday

18 Saturday

19 Sunday

Hydrangea azisai [now *Hydrangea macrophylla* 'Azisai']. Hand-coloured engraving after H. Popp from
Philipp Franz von Siebold & J. G. Zuccarini, *Flora Japonica* (1835–41).

October

2008
WEEK 4

20 Monday

21 Tuesday

Jewish Festival of Tabernacles (Succoth), Eighth Day
Last Quarter

22 Wednesday

23 Thursday

24 Friday

United Nations Day

25 Saturday

26 Sunday

British Summertime ends

Aria ellipsoidea [now *Sorbus aria*]. Hand-coloured engraving after C. Delorme from Alexis Jordan & Jules Fourreau, *Icones ad floram Europae* (1866–1903).

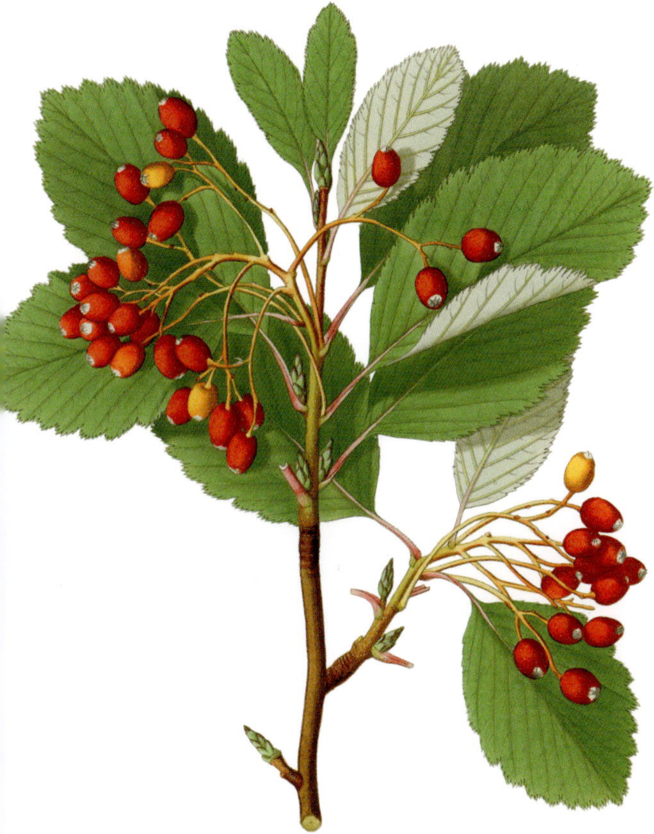

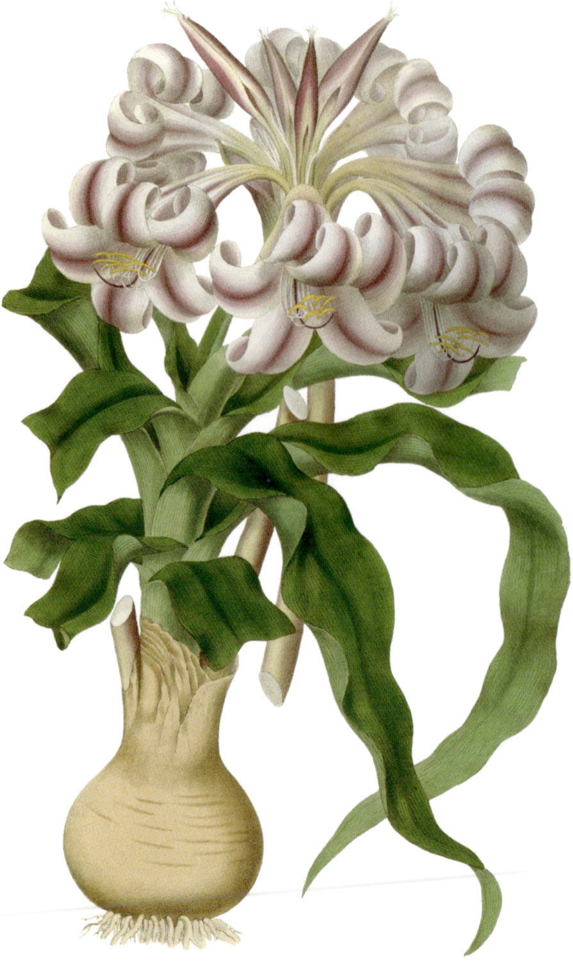

October & November

2008
WEEK 44

27 Monday

Holiday, Republic of Ireland
Holiday, New Zealand (Labour Day)

28 Tuesday

New Moon

29 Wednesday

30 Thursday

31 Friday

Hallowe'en

1 Saturday

All Saints' Day

2 Sunday

Crinum zeylanicum. Hand-coloured engraving after Vishnupersaud from Nathaniel Wallich, *Plantae Asiaticae rariores* (1829–32), believed to have been coloured by John Clark.

November

2008
WEEK 4

3 Monday

---

4 Tuesday

---

5 Wednesday

Guy Fawkes' Day

6 Thursday

First Quarter

7 Friday

---

8 Saturday

---

9 Sunday

Remembrance Sunday, UK

Leycesteria formosa. Hand-coloured engraving after Gorachand from Nathaniel Wallich, *Plantae Asiaticae rariores* (1829–32), believed to have been coloured by John Clark.

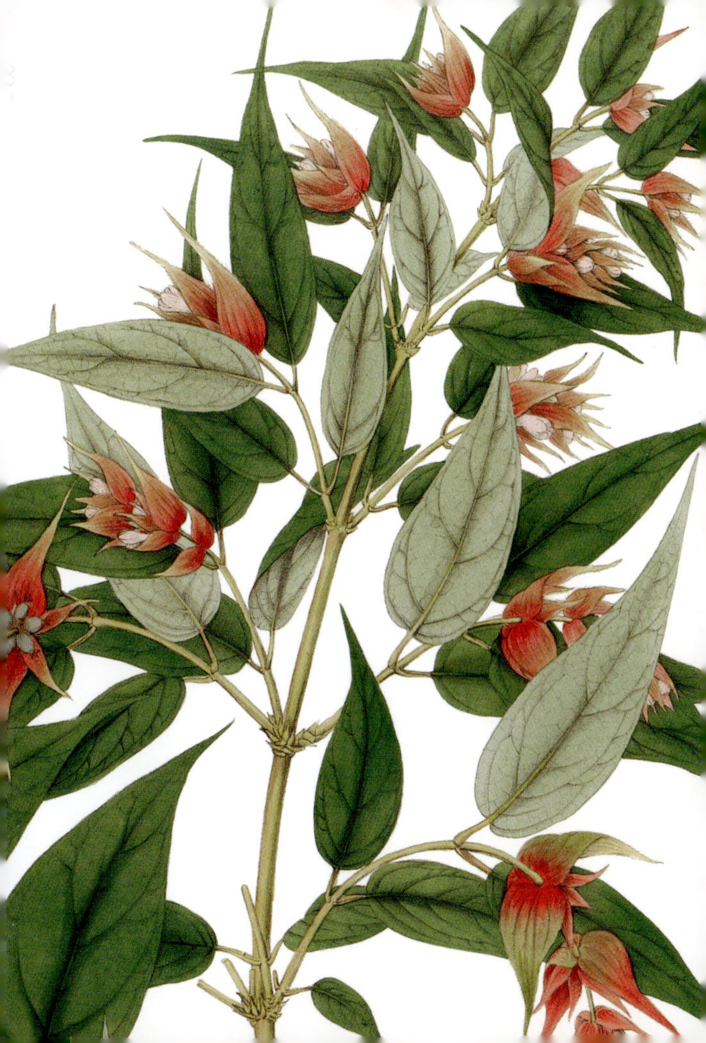

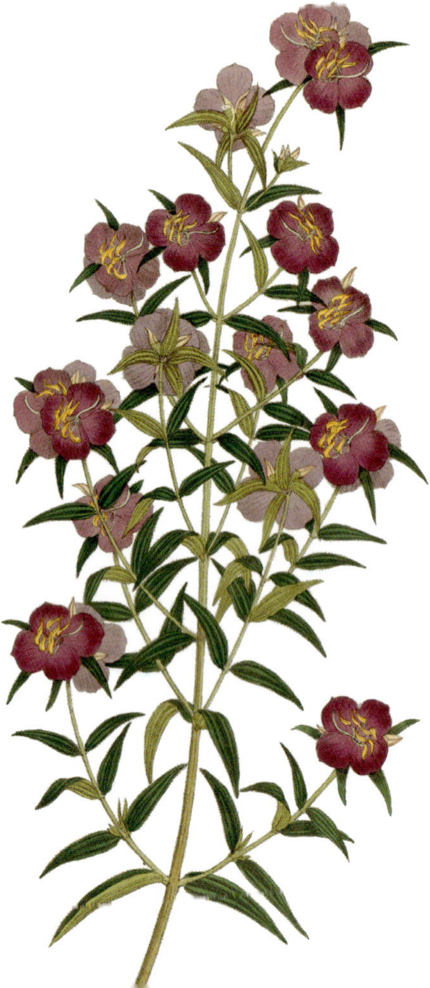

November

2008
WEEK 46

---

10 Monday

---

11 Tuesday

Holiday, Canada (Remembrance Day)
and USA (Veteran's Day)

---

12 Wednesday

---

13 Thursday

Full Moon

---

14 Friday

RHS London Flower Show

---

15 Saturday

RHS London Flower Show

---

16 Sunday

Osbeckia angustifolia [now *Osbeckia chinensis* var. *angustifolia*]. Hand-coloured engraving after Gorachand from Nathaniel Wallich, *Plantae Asiaticae rariores* (1829–32), believed to have been coloured by John Clark.

November

2008
WEEK 47

---

17 Monday

---

18 Tuesday

---

19 Wednesday

Last Quarter

20 Thursday

---

21 Friday

---

22 Saturday

---

23 Sunday

Meyenia hawtayneana. Hand-coloured engraving after Gorachand from Nathaniel Wallich,
Plantae Asiaticae rariores (1829–32), believed to have been coloured by John Clark.

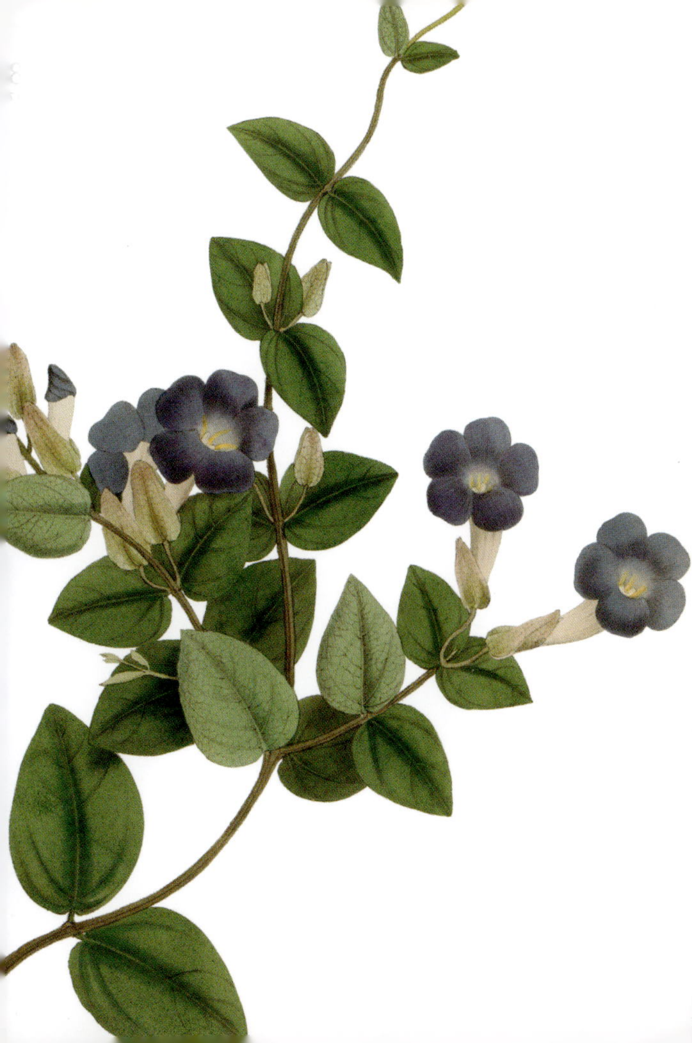

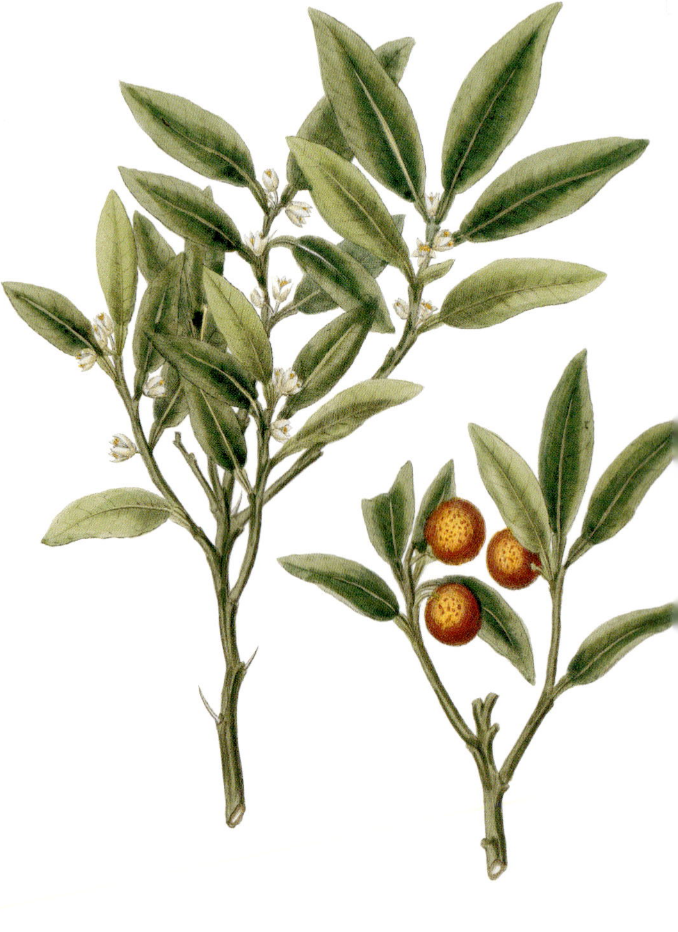

November

2008
WEEK 48

24 Monday

25 Tuesday

26 Wednesday

27 Thursday

Holiday, USA (Thanksgiving Day)
New Moon

28 Friday

29 Saturday

30 Sunday

Advent Sunday
St Andrew's Day

Fortunella japonica. Hand-coloured engraving after H. Popp from Philipp Franz von Siebold & J. G. Zuccarini, *Flora Japonica* (1835–41).

December

2008
WEEK 4

1 Monday

2 Tuesday

3 Wednesday

4 Thursday

5 Friday

First Quarter

6 Saturday

7 Sunday

Corylus avellana. Unsigned hand-coloured engraving from H. G. L. Reichenbach et al.,
Icones florae Germanicae et Helveticae, vol. 12 (1850).

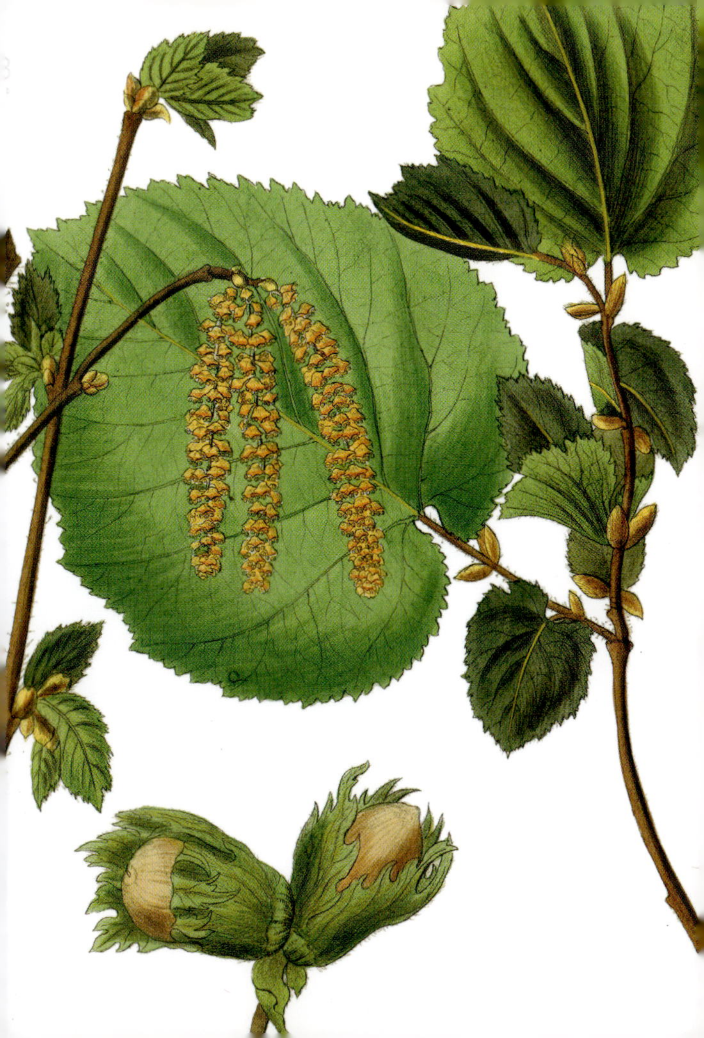

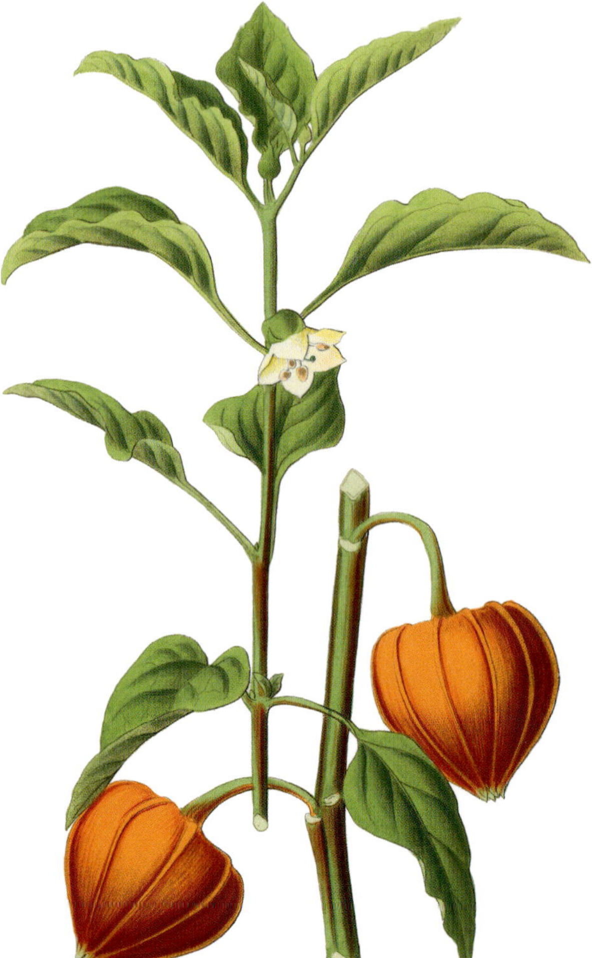

December

2008
WEEK 50

8 Monday

9 Tuesday

10 Wednesday

11 Thursday

12 Friday

Full Moon

13 Saturday

14 Sunday

Physalis alkekengi. Hand-coloured engraving after H. G. Reichenbach from H. G. L. Reichenbach et al., *Icones florae Germanicae et Helveticae*, vol. 20 (1861).

December

2008
WEEK 51

15 Monday

16 Tuesday

17 Wednesday

18 Thursday

19 Friday

Last Quarter

20 Saturday

21 Sunday

Winter Solstice

Viscum album. Hand-coloured engraving after F. G. Kohl from H. G. L. Reichenbach et al., *Icones florae Germanicae et Helveticae*, vol. 24 (1908).

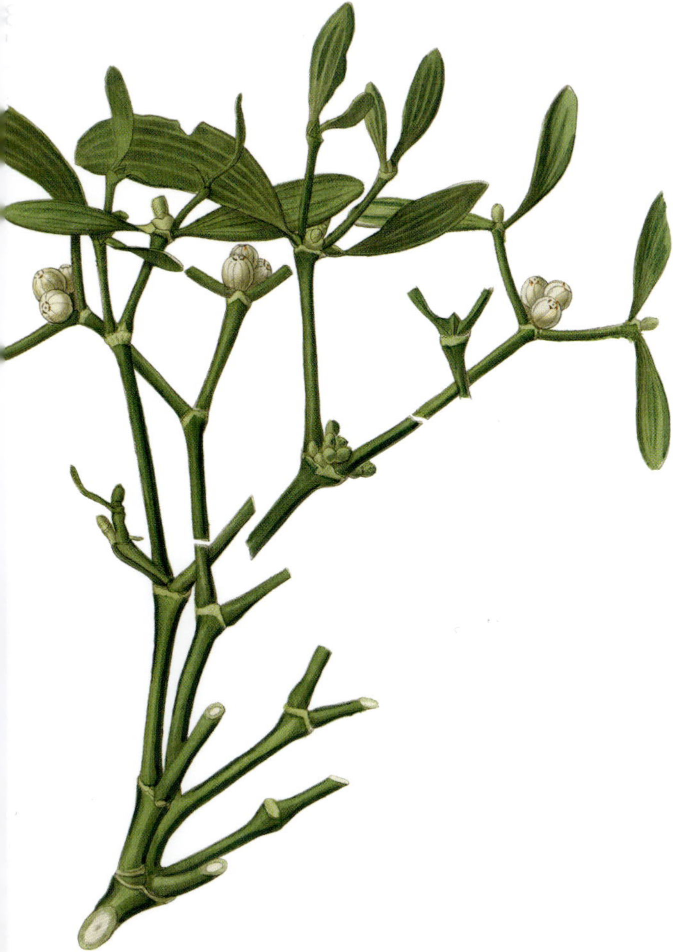

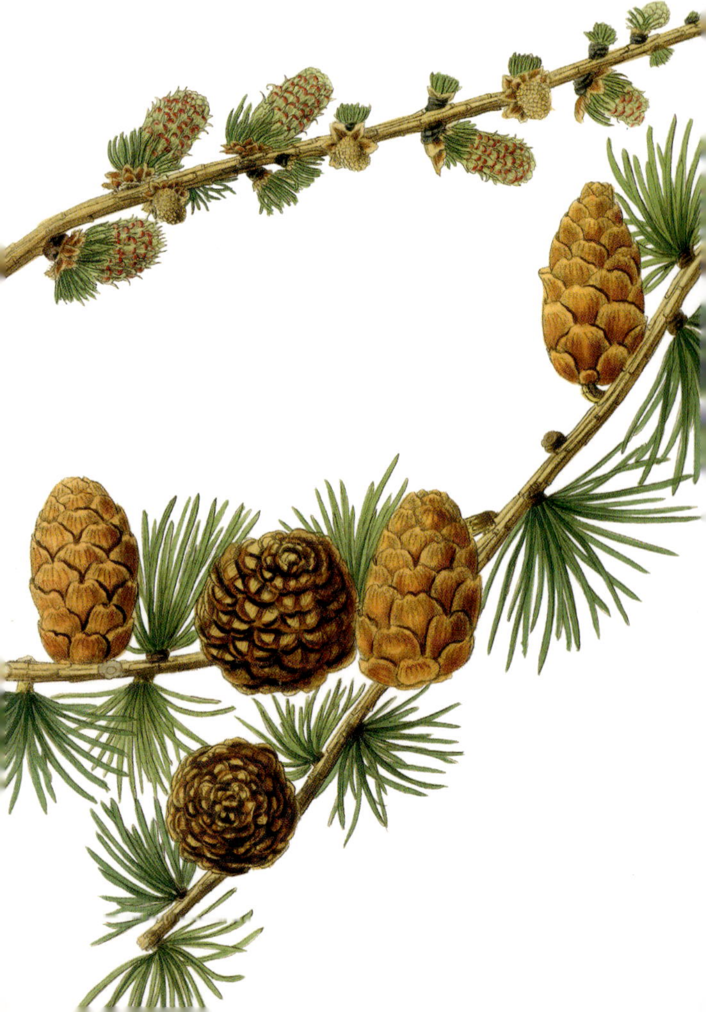

December

2008
WEEK 52

22 Monday

Jewish Festival of Chanukah, First Day

23 Tuesday

24 Wednesday

Christmas Eve

25 Thursday

Christmas Day
Holiday, UK, Republic of Ireland, Canada,
USA, Australia and New Zealand

26 Friday

Boxing Day (St Stephen's Day)
Holiday, UK, Republic of Ireland, Canada, Australia and New Zealand

27 Saturday

New Moon

28 Sunday

Larix europaea [now *Larix decidua*]. Unsigned hand-coloured engraving from H. G. L. Reichenbach et al., *Icones florae Germanicae et Helveticae*, vol. 11 (1849).

December & January

2009
WEEK 1

29 Monday

Islamic New Year (subject to sighting of the moon)

30 Tuesday

31 Wednesday

New Year's Eve

1 Thursday

New Year's Day
Holiday, UK, Republic or Ireland, Canada,
USA, Australia and New Zealand

2 Friday

Holiday, Scotland and New Zealand

3 Saturday

4 Sunday

First Quarter

Myristica amygdalina [now *Horsfieldia amygdalina*]. Hand-coloured engraving after Vishnupersaud from Nathaniel Wallich, *Plantae Asiaticae rariores* (1829–32), believed to have been coloured by John Clark.

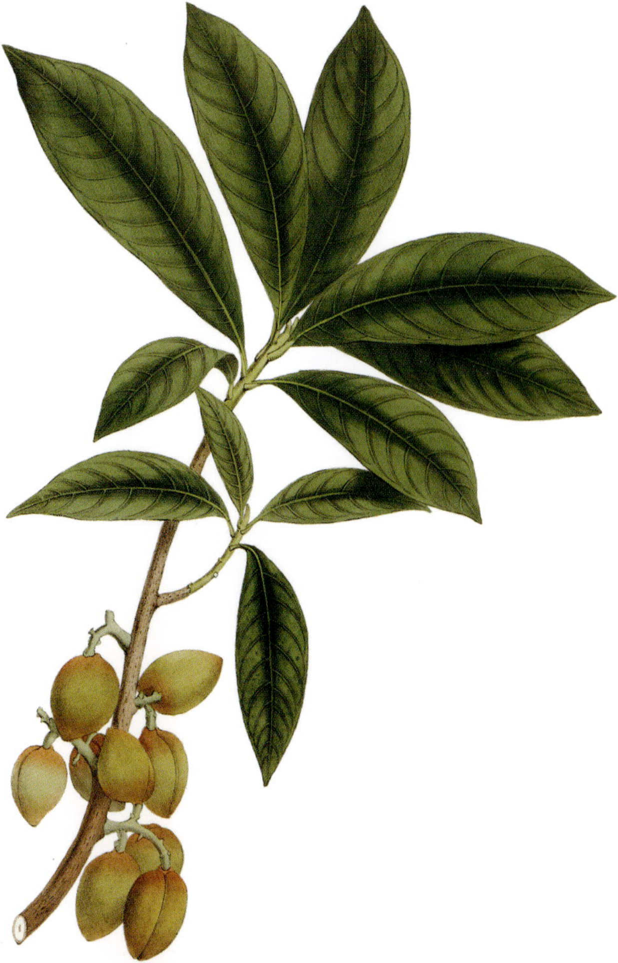

EUROPEAN NATIONAL HOLIDAYS 2008

AUSTRIA	JAN. 1, 6; MARCH 23, 24; MAY 1, 11, 12, 22; AUG. 15; OCT. 26; NOV. 1; DEC. 8, 25, 26
BELGIUM	JAN. 1; MARCH 23, 24; MAY 1, 11, 12; JULY 11, 21; AUG. 15; NOV. 1, 11, 15; DEC. 25, 26
BULGARIA	JAN. 1; MARCH 3; APRIL 27, 28; MAY 1, 6, 24; SEPT. 6, 22; NOV. 1; DEC. 24, 25, 26.
CYPRUS	JAN. 1, 6; MARCH 10, 25; APRIL 1, 25, 27, 28; MAY 1, JUNE 15, 16; AUG. 15; OCT. 1, 28; DEC. 25, 26
CZECH REPUBLIC	JAN. 1; MARCH 23, 24; MAY 1, 8; JULY 5, 6; SEPT. 28; OCT. 28; NOV. 17; DEC. 24, 25, 26
DENMARK	JAN. 1; MARCH 20, 21, 23, 24; APRIL 18; MAY 1, 11, 12; JUNE 5; DEC. 25, 26
ESTONIA	JAN. 1; FEB. 24; MARCH 21, 23; MAY 1, 11; JUNE 23, 24; AUG. 20; DEC. 24, 25, 26
FINLAND	JAN. 1, 6; MARCH 21, 23, 24; MAY 1, 11; JUNE 21; NOV. 1; DEC. 6, 25, 26
FRANCE	JAN. 1; MARCH 21, 23, 24; MAY 1, 8, 11, 12; JULY 14; AUG. 15; NOV. 1, 11; DEC. 25
GERMANY	JAN. 1, 6; MARCH 21, 23, 24; MAY 1, 11, 12, 22; AUG. 15; OCT. 3, 31; NOV. 1, 19; DEC. 25, 26
GREECE	JAN. 1, 6; MARCH 10, 25; APRIL 25, 27, 28; MAY 1; JUNE 15, 16; AUG. 15; OCT. 28; DEC. 25, 26
HUNGARY	JAN. 1; MARCH 15, 23, 24; MAY 1, 11, 12; AUG. 20; OCT. 23; NOV. 1; DEC. 25, 26
ITALY	JAN. 1, 6; MARCH 23, 24; APRIL 25; MAY 1; JUNE 2; AUG. 15; NOV. 1; DEC. 8, 25, 26
LATVIA	JAN. 1; MARCH 21, 23, 24; MAY 1, 4; JUNE 23, 24; NOV. 18; DEC. 25, 26, 31
LITHUANIA	JAN. 1; FEB. 16, 18; MARCH 11, 23, 24, 25; MAY 1, 4, 5; JUNE 24; JULY 6, 7; AUG. 15; NOV. 1, 3; DEC. 25, 26
LUXEMBOURG	JAN. 1; FEB. 4; MARCH 23, 24; MAY 1, 11, 12; JUNE 23; AUG. 15; SEPT. 1; NOV. 1; DEC. 25, 26
MALTA	JAN. 1; FEB. 10; MARCH 19, 21, 23, 31; MAY 1; JUNE 7, 29; AUG. 15; SEPT. 8, 21; DEC. 8, 13, 25
NETHERLANDS	JAN. 1; MARCH 21, 23, 24; APRIL 30; MAY 1, 11, 12; DEC. 25, 26
NORWAY	JAN. 1; MARCH 20, 21, 23, 24; MAY 1, 11, 12, 17; DEC. 25, 26
POLAND	JAN. 1; MARCH 23, 24; MAY 1, 3, 22; AUG. 15; NOV. 1, 11; DEC. 25, 26
PORTUGAL	JAN. 1; FEB. 5; MARCH 21, 23, 24; APRIL 25; MAY 1, 22; JUNE 10, 13; AUG. 15; OCT. 5; NOV. 1, 8, 25; DEC. 1, 8, 25
ROMANIA	JAN. 1, 2; APRIL 27, 28; MAY 1; DEC. 1, 25, 26
SLOVAKIA	JAN. 1, 6; MARCH 21, 23, 24; MAY 1, 8; JULY 5; AUG. 29; SEPT. 1, 15; NOV. 1, 17; DEC. 24, 25, 26
SLOVENIA	JAN. 1, 2; FEB. 8; MARCH 23, 24; APRIL 27; MAY 1, 2, 11; JUNE 25; AUG. 15; OCT. 31; NOV. 1; DEC. 25, 26
SPAIN	JAN. 1, 6; MARCH 19, 20, 21, 23, 24; MAY 1, 11, 22; JULY 25; AUG. 15; OCT. 12; NOV. 1; DEC. 6, 8, 25, 26
SWEDEN	JAN. 1, 6; MARCH 21,23, 24; MAY 1, 11; JUNE 6, 21; NOV. 1; DEC. 25, 26
SWITZERLAND	JAN. 1, 2; MARCH 21, 23, 24; MAY 1, 11, 12; AUG. 1, 15; NOV. 1; DEC. 8, 25, 26